MW00834589

500
PRAYERS

for CATHOLIC SCHOOLS & PARISH YOUTH GROUPS

Filomena Tassi and Peter Tassi

TWENTY-THIRD PUBLICATIONS

185 WILLOW STREET • PO BOX 180 • MYSTIC, CT 06355
TEL: 1-800-321-0411 • FAX: 1-800-572-0788
E-MAIL: ttpubs@aol.com • www.twentythirdpublications.com

Twenty-Third Publications
A Division of Bayard
185 Willow Street
P.O. Box 180
Mystic, CT 06355
(860) 536-2611 or (800) 321-0411
www.twentythirdpublications.com
ISBN:1-58595-340-7

Library of Congress Catalog Card Number: 2004102647
Printed in the U.S.A.

Dedication

We dedicate this work of love to Father Lou Quinn, Scarboro Foreign Missionary priest in the Dominican Republic. His tireless work for the poor and his endless accomplishments over the past forty years have inspired people throughout the world. His accomplishments are so immense; he motivates all of us to "pick up our shovel" and begin. He teaches us that dreams can come true and all things are possible when everything we do is done for love of others. Thank you, Father Lou, for teaching us to live out our prayers.

Acknowledgments

Thank you to John Valvasori and Nat Gallo for their strong Christian leadership and their ongoing support and encouragement. To the students and staff at St. Thomas More and St. Mary's Catholic Secondary Schools in Hamilton, who inspire us in our work and our own personal prayer.

Thank you to Mallory Salas, who spent endless hours typing and collating the initial drafts of this book. Thank you to Father Leo Walsh for his theological guidance, his prudent advice, and his spiritual support and encouragement.

Contents

Introduction

For many years, we have been asked by teachers, students, and parents in our school community for an all-encompassing, daily prayer book. The prayer book would include many different prayers, such as daily prayers; prayers for saints days, liturgical seasons, special occasions, and specific themes; prayers based on the historical life and teachings of Jesus; and traditional prayers. Although many prayer books were available, they did not satisfy the need for the inclusive and comprehensive resource our community was seeking. Consequently, we wrote this book.

Schools can use these prayers to begin their day, and teachers can use them to begin a class. They are also helpful for families to use to celebrate each day with a special prayer. Not only does this book have a different prayer for each day of the school year, it is an educational tool, teaching young people about the lives of the saints, the liturgical season, feast days, and memorial days. Through prayer, it gives them an understanding of the life and teachings of Jesus based on the Gospel of Matthew. In addition, this book offers prayers based on specific themes, events throughout the year, and all of the traditional prayers.

We wrote this book so that it would accommodate young children, teenagers and adults. You can adapt the prayers to meet your particular needs, and to suit a certain age group. It is our hope that the prayers will be an inspiration to all people.

We are grateful to the teachers, students, and many others who provided us with direction to write this book to accommodate their needs. We give thanks to God for the gift of all these people and for the direction and inspiration of the Holy Spirit in writing these prayers.

CHAPTER ONE

Daily Prayers

Dear God, be with each of us this day. Help us take a moment to feel your presence, and the strength and courage you provide. May your presence lift our hearts and our souls and enable us to direct all our actions toward you. Help us be faith-filled people as we carry out your great work today. Amen.

Dear God, help each of us use the gifts you have blessed us with to enhance this community. May we be willing to give of ourselves, as Mary, the Mother of Jesus did, to make this community one we can all be proud of. In giving we will attain greatness, for in this way your love is revealed through each and every one of us. Amen.

Dear God, keep us strong so that we can carry out your works: feeding the hungry, visiting the sick, clothing the naked, and being a voice for those who suffer persecution. Bless us this year, so that we may all experience rich friendships, authentic success, and purpose in all we do. Amen.

Dear God, we thank you for our families, for those who provide care for us. We pray for the families who struggle to find food and shelter. May the support that we lend brighten their days and comfort their nights. If one day we are in their place, may we be willing to accept the love and generosity of others. Amen.

Dear God, give us the strength to reach out to others in need. May each of us discover our gifts and use them to make the lives of others a little easier. May we always be willing to make sacrifices for the benefit of our fellow human beings and do this in loving service to one another as Jesus taught us. Amen.

Dear God, may we take time today to search within ourselves and see the gifts you have blessed us with. May we not be jealous of the gifts of others, but nurture and celebrate our own gifts. In giving of ourselves we say thank you God, from whom all our gifts come. Amen.

Good and gracious God, it is good to have ambition and to strive for goals. However, when we expect too much of ourselves and of others, we can drive others away and we ourselves can feel a lack of meaning in our lives. We must be more accepting of who we are and who others are. Though this is not easy, by accepting who we are with all our weaknesses, may we have inner peace and make room for everyone in our life. May we see ourselves and others as your children and treat everyone accordingly. Amen.

Dear God, help each of us recognize the power we have to help make a difference in this world. Let us not be disheartened by cynicism and complacency. Let us recognize the power of our actions. May they serve as an example to others and bring them out of their suffering and despair. Amen.

Loving God, bless each of us today. Help us nourish a deep faith that brings us closer to you with each passing day. As we open our hearts and minds to your love, may all our words and actions be a living witness to the wonderful love you have for us. Amen.

Dear God, help us this day reflect on our priorities as we gain knowledge and experience. May we take time to evaluate our values and how we live them each day. May we recognize that learning goes on throughout our entire lives, and that there is much to be learned both academically and through personal experience. May we learn by our mistakes, progress through our successes, and share our wisdom. Help us dream unceasingly, and give us the strength, courage, and wisdom to never stop following our dreams. Amen.

Dear God, help us see today the wonderful gifts with which we have been blessed. Help us discover the hidden talents and skills we possess. May we recognize our potential and never underestimate all we can achieve. Help us continue to dream and explore and never give up! We ask this through Jesus, Our Lord and Savior. Amen.

Loving God, sometimes there seems little in our world today to offer hope for our future. We pray for all our students, that they may be creative and reflective thinkers. May they take what they have learned and develop it in a way that leads to discoveries—discoveries that help us live to our fullest potential; discoveries that embrace the values of Jesus in all the areas of science and learning. May we be wise in our reflection and analysis. May we have the foresight to recognize consequences, the courage to take a stand, and the faith to keep us open to the Holy Spirit. In this way we can see a future filled with hope, a hope that looks forward to the creativity, discovery, and implementation of the gifts you have given us. Amen.

Dear God, give us the courage and strength today to carry out your will. May we keep an open heart and mind, and listen to the voice of the Holy Spirit. When life presents us with challenges that consume us, let us know that you are always present with us. May we feel the comfort of your unconditional love. Keep us strong and confident in all that we say and do. Amen.

Creator God, help us as we learn. May we have the discipline to devote ourselves to our academic studies. Help us take what we learn and apply it to our lives. May our knowledge be used to serve you, dear God, as we reach out to others and make the lives of those who struggle around us a little easier. Amen.

God of hope, as we strive to deepen our relationship with you, help each of us become involved in activities that lead us closer to you. Recognizing our uniqueness, may we learn to appreciate the people and practices that make our faith life more profound. May we have the wisdom and courage to nurture these relationships and value the true gift they are to us. May we feel the peace, happiness, and love you offer us, and may these be a source of strength and encouragement as we journey through life. Amen.

God of justice, help us promote the dignity of each and every person. May we use our gifts to work for justice. In a world that often embraces values that run contrary to the gospel, may we each speak and act in a way reflects the work and actions of your Son Jesus. Help us respect diversity and be open to learn and grow from the contributions made by other cultures and faiths. While recognizing the importance of freedom may we never compromise our gospel values, and may we always work toward attaining the common good. Amen.

Dear God, disturb us when we become too comfortable. Give us the courage to take a stand when we witness acts of injustice. Motivate us when we become complacent. In moments of self-doubt let us know the power and strength of your love. Amen.

God of our journey, be with us today as we journey toward you. May we always feel your presence in our lives. When life's challenges seem overwhelming, let us know that you are with us. When we need support and comfort to go the extra mile, let your love fill us and nourish us. May we be stewards of your love, making your Word known to others in all we say and do. Amen.

God of wisdom, we face many decisions in our lives. We pray for the prudence to make choices that assist us in developing our full potential. We pray for the strength to face difficult challenges and obstacles. We pray for wisdom so that we look not only at the immediate future, but consider the long-term effect of our decisions. We pray for wonderful friendships, so that we may have the comfort of supportive and loyal friends. Finally, we pray that we always remain open to the Spirit, whose voice can be heard in our hearts. Amen.

Dear God of light, may we be surrounded by people who bring out the light within us, and who inspire us to make that light shine. We pray that, in sharing our gifts, others will witness our light and recognize its brilliance as being rooted in Jesus. May our works, actions, and contributions help others come to know the power of Jesus' love and lead all into a deeper relationship with him. Amen.

Dear God, may each of us appreciate our families and work toward nurturing strong family relationships. Help us better understand those in our family and respect their decisions. Help us find creative and effective ways to improve communication with one another so we can better understand and respond to the daily issues that arise in family life. May we show compassion and love to all we encounter on a daily basis so that those who do not experience the power of love in their homes may come to know what love is. Amen.

Dear God, there are many people who have gone before us and have demonstrated great courage, including the saints and martyrs. We often see acts of courage in our community, in our families, and among our friends. Today we pray that each of us be granted the courage we need to live our life with dignity and respect. Amen.

Dear God, give us the confidence to trust in ourselves knowing that you dwell within us. Enable us to discover who we are, knowing that we are made in your image. Give us the strength to respond to your voice, knowing that you call each of us by name. Amen.

God of peace, may each of us be instruments of your peace. Help us be aware of the many opportunities we have to promote peace and justice. May we recognize that the simplest of actions can make a difference in the lives of those around us. May we never underestimate the power of our actions. Help us know how best to promote peace and justice. Amen.

Heavenly Father, giver of all good gifts, look with love on these students in our school community. Bless their lives and help them reflect Christ's love for all people. Fill them with your love, and let them bring your light into our community. Give them the strength to serve all those in need. Give them the courage to stand strong for what is right, and the wisdom to discover your goodness in all things. Father, we give you praise and glory as we ask this through Christ our Lord, in the love of your Spirit, now and forever. Amen.

Dear God, bless each of us in our vocation as learners, as disciples. May we be willing to accept the invitation that Jesus offers with his powerful words: "Come, follow me." May all our choices reflect a positive response to this invitation, and may we each be true disciples of Jesus Christ. Amen.

Dear God, recognizing that we are made in your image and likeness, grant each of us the courage to be who you made us to be. May our compassion enable us to reach out and assist others in need. May our convictions enable us to stand up for what is important to us. May our sensitivity enable us to recognize cries for help. May our concern for others enable us to get involved. May our faith enable us to declare that all we do, we do in your name. Amen.

Loving God, as we progress through this year may we be granted the sense of balance necessary to fulfill all that is asked of us. May we take the time to evaluate what we do and ensure that our priorities are in the proper order. Help us let go of what we can let go of, and become involved in what brings peace and happiness to ourselves and others. We ask this through Jesus our Lord and Savior. Amen.

Dear God, it is not always easy to be courageous. When someone does something wrong, it is often easier to let it pass and not take a stand. When people are blamed for something they did not do, it is often easier to say nothing. Today we pray for the courage to right the wrong, to take a stand, and to take a risk. In so doing we can be satisfied with who we are and what we are about. We gain peace and a sense of happiness that can only be attained through our acts of courage. Give us this kind of courage. Amen.

Dear God, help each of us adopt practices that help us live out the most important commandment: to love you, ourselves, and our neighbor. Free us from attitudes and behaviors that restrict our ability to love. Instead, may we remain open to the Spirit so that we can grow closer to God. May we follow the direction of the Spirit with strength and be mindful of the invitation Jesus offers to each of us: "Come, follow me." Amen.

God of blessings, we give you thanks for the many wonderful things you have blessed us with. May we always recognize and appreciate all that we have. May we take time to see beauty in the simple things that surround us. May we never lose sight of our blessings. May they be a source of strength when we experience difficult times. Amen.

Dear Lord, you taught us that in weakness there is strength, in defeat there is victory, in the cross there is the resurrection. With this teaching, we come to see the beauty in ourselves and in others. We accept ourselves and others for who we are. With this teaching help us learn to love ourselves and others, and forgive each other our faults and failings. Amen.

Dear God, we thank you for the many gifts you have given us. We know that all our blessings come from you. Help each of us take time to recognize our gifts, and work toward developing these gifts. May we be willing to reach out to others and share all that we have been blessed with. It is in helping others that we gain joy and fulfillment here on earth. Amen.

Dear God, we know that change is a constant in our lives. It is not always easy to change, even when it may be necessary for our growth and development. Help us remain open, reflect on our ways, and ask if there are things we can do to help deepen our relationship with you. Amen.

Dear Lord, thank you for the gift of true companionship. In the darkest moments of our lives you send us a friend to bring your healing love. In times of joy you send a friend to celebrate our joy. In times of sorrow you send a friend for us to lean on. Help us support and comfort one another and always be willing to reach out in times of need. Amen.

Crucified Lord, life is not always easy. There are moments when we feel helpless, overwhelmed, and defeated. Help us recognize that suffering is sometimes part of life. We do not know why we must suffer; we do know, however, that suffering enables us to see the world in a new way. In and through this new vision may we be better able to help those in need. Amen.

Dear God, may you be a source of hope within us. May our belief in you fill us with confidence and joy as we face life's challenges. May we remain open to the Spirit who will guide us in ways of love and peace. Amen.

Drew

Dear God, give us the courage to take the road less travelled, the determination to create our own path, and the wisdom that results in following our own trail. Amen.

Loving God, we pray today for the courage to stand up for what we believe in. Grant us the insight to find solutions that promote gospel values, and the leadership to encourage others to embrace those values. May we never underestimate the power of our actions and recognize that we are instruments of your love and compassion. Amen.

Good and gracious God, you are the giver of all good things. You provide the rain for the harvest and the sun for the flowers. You created the moon and stars to light the night sky, and the mountains and hillsides to beautify the day. May we always be mindful that everything is possible to you. We need only place our entire self in your love and care to know that all will be well. Amen.

Dear God, let us open our hearts to you and work toward deepening our relationship with you. May we recognize the wonderful blessings that faith has to offer, the great works we can accomplish with faith, and the peace a strong faith life brings. May we each grow in our faith. Amen.

Dear God, we thank you for all your blessings. We know that all our gifts come from you. May we always give of ourselves. May we use our gifts in a way that shows our gratitude for them. Amen.

Creator God, help us pay attention to our minds and bodies. Let us treat our bodies and minds with respect, knowing that we are made in your image and likeness. May we always recognize that with your help we have the ability to accomplish great things. May we dream unceasingly and have the confidence, courage, and determination to follow our dreams. Amen.

Daily Prayers

Dear God, as we search within ourselves to discover our vocation, the path our lives are to take, help us come to know who we truly are. May we not be misled by the pressures around us as we make decisions about our lives. May our decisions be rooted in an understanding of who we are, what our gifts are, and where our deepest desire lies. In doing so we can discover who we are and what we can offer the world. Amen.

Mr Lonteen's GM

Dear God, may we treasure each day. Help us never take life or time for granted. May we always be enthusiastic about life and about what we do with our time. When life begins to lose its meaning for us, give us the strength to seek out guidance, new beginnings, new directions, and new paths. We ask this through Christ, the Lord. Amen.

Loving God, grant us the faith that enables us to let go of whatever brings us down. Give us the strength to confront the issues we need to confront, and the wisdom to find the solutions that lead us and others closer to you. May we always trust in the love and support you offer, and may this keep us optimistic and hopeful as we face each day. Amen.

Dear God, grant us the faith and insight to recognize the way to peace and happiness. We know that your way is the way to Truth. Help us each day to know your way and to follow you. May we always listen to the voice of the Spirit within our hearts. Amen.

Dear God, it is not always easy to keep our hearts and minds focused on the gospel message. We are bombarded with cultural messages that undermine gospel values. Help us remain strong in faith and live out the gospel by treating others with dignity and respect. We know that in dying to ourselves we will be granted eternal peace and happiness. Amen.

Loving God, we give you thanks for the many blessings in our lives. In times of trial, let us remember our blessings. Help us focus on whatever raises our spirits and offers us comfort. In times of despair may we cling to your love, and may it bring us closer to you. Amen.

Dear God, sometimes it is tempting to give in to negative thoughts, doubting ourselves, and living with a poor self-image. Yet you challenge us to choose positive thoughts and actions, to believe in ourselves, and use our gifts wisely. This choice holds more responsibilities but leads to a more fulfilling life. Bless and guide our thoughts and actions throughout this day that we may draw ever closer to you. Amen.

God of all, we choose you. We have been created in your image, in infinite beauty, wisdom, and love. We give you thanks for creating us, and for all creation. Continue to encourage us, inspire us, and strengthen us to always make the right choice—the choice for you. Amen.

Dear God, may we always recognize you as the source of our gifts. Help us to develop them in full appreciation of your love for us. Keep us strong so we may have the will power and discipline to make the sacrifices necessary to be the best we can be. Help us remember those who need our time and talents. May we be willing to share them for the benefit of others. Amen.

God our Savior, help us recognize the opportunities we are given each day to make a difference in the lives of those around us. Give us the insight and the confidence to seize these opportunities. May we feel the peace that comes with bringing justice to others. May we feel the comfort that comes with reaching out to others. By believing in ourselves and in our abilities help us make a difference in the world. Amen.

God of strength, the challenges we face each day are not always easy. Some days we feel as if we may not be able to handle all that is expected of us. Help each of us maintain a sense of calm in the storm that surrounds us. May our faith and love for you provide us with an inner peace that enables us to handle all situations in a calm and efficient manner. Amen.

Creator God, inspire us to see you in the beauty of nature. Help us recognize your infinite love and power as we watch the changes each season brings. May we always see the beauty in your creation and know that, with trust in you, all things are possible. Amen.

Dear God, being human means that we have many weaknesses. Help us not to expect perfection from ourselves but recognize that only Jesus is perfect. May we try to improve what we are capable of improving and look to Jesus as a model and a guide. Help us be satisfied with our personal best and know that this is all you expect from us. Amen.

Dear God, help us to be compassionate and loving people. As we journey through the day, encourage us to reach out to someone who needs our help. Help us know when a simple act can make a big difference in the life of someone. May we see the face of Jesus in everyone and share his love with all. Amen.

Loving God, help us this day to do our best in work and play. We know that we cannot do everything. Help us focus on the wonderful work that we can do. We are called to do all that we can and to leave the rest in your hands. We pray that your grace will touch all of our works today. Amen.

Dear Lord, you give each of us tremendous resources on which we can rely. You have given us courage, prudence, intelligence, and hope. Help us use these virtues to serve others and help build your kingdom. Amen.

Dear Jesus, we sometimes face situations where values we embrace are called into question. Help each of us become passionate about the values you lived and taught us. Grant us the courage to stand up for what we believe and to make the necessary sacrifices to ensure that your teaching is never compromised. Amen.

4/24
Tues

Dear Lord, we thank you for the blessing of our friends. They enrich our lives with compassion and understanding; they touch our hearts with devotion and love. Friends watch over us and walk beside us. May we always appreciate the friends who give us the support and encouragement we need to discover our talents and gifts. Amen.

Dear Lord, we know that you live within us, and we need only look within ourselves to find you. We are capable of great works, and we can make a difference in the world around us. May we never doubt ourselves or our abilities, knowing that all things are possible through faith and love in you. Amen.

Give us, O Lord, the perception we need to look within ourselves and discover the beauty and gifts we possess. Give us the courage to show others the talents they have. Help us serve others in the community and in so doing build up your kingdom. We ask this through Jesus, our Lord. Amen.

You call us by name, compassionate God, to comfort those who are upset, to reach out to the hungry, to embrace the outcast, to respond to tragedies. May we always be sensitive to the needs of others and be willing to do what we can to make their lives easier. May our giving be endless, and may our joy in giving bring us great peace. We ask this through Jesus, who sacrificed much and gained everything. Amen.

Dear God, there are times when we are put to the test, but fear and apprehension take control and prevent us from taking action. There are times when our failures take hold of us and immobilize us. We pray today for discipline to focus on our inner strength, the infinite reservoir of talents and gifts within, and use these to build your kingdom. Help us see, Lord, that you are always with us. Amen.

Teach us to be humble and compassionate, O Lord. When we are tempted to judge others, let us turn our attention inward. When we are ready to accuse others, let us take another look at the situation. When we form opinions about others, keep us open to further reflection. May we always be willing to take the time to walk in the shoes of another. Amen.

Thurs 4/26

Dear God, may we have the strength and devotion to discover what we are passionate about. May we always keep an open heart and mind and be willing to listen and learn from the experience of others. Help us discover the things that cause our hearts to beat strongly. May we be granted the courage to pursue these passions and the faith to make your Word known to everyone in all that we do. Amen.

God of love and of life, let us take time to look deep within ourselves and discover the gifts you have blessed us with. May we take the time to direct our lives in a way that best uses our own unique combination of gifts. May our education help us discover where our strengths and interests lie. May our faith guide us in realizing our gifts. May we always be open to the direction of the Spirit and never forget the love you have for each of us. Amen.

Dwell among us, O Lord. Help us make your presence known to others. Give us the patience and guidance to come to know your will for us, and to carry it out day by day. May the example of Jesus always inspire and encourage us as we journey closer to you, God of all. Amen.

Dear Jesus, grant us the courage to defend those who are bullied, to speak up when discrimination occurs, to step in when the marginalized are teased or ridiculed, to open a door for someone who is struggling to open it themselves. In these small gestures great love is demonstrated; in these small gestures we show others the face of God. Amen.

Mon 4/23

Dear God, help each of us to remember that life is a gift. May we take time today to tell our family and friends just how much we care about each one of them. May we live each moment as a gift and know that you, O Lord, are always with us, encouraging us to appreciate all that we have. Amen.

We thank you, O God, for all those who are with us in love and service—the people who put our needs before their needs, who are sensitive to our every response and reaction, and who reach out to us when we are troubled or upset. May they always be blessed with the peace that comes from knowing their work is appreciated. May they be blessed with happiness as they share so fully in the joys we share and blessed with the love they so readily give. Amen.

Dear God, today let us reflect on our relationship with you. We know that you are the way to peace and happiness, yet it is often difficult to take time to discover the way to you. Help each of us make this a priority in our lives and recognize that the better we come to know you and accept you the more happiness and peace our lives will hold. Amen.

How can we better serve you, O Lord? How can we make your Word known to all whom we meet each day? May we gladly take every opportunity to bring your love and your peace to all people. Amen.

Loving God, there are many opportunities to raise the spirit of our community. May we not see this as a responsibility for others, but as something *we* can and should do. May each of us try to better the lives of everyone with whom we live and work. May we approach this task with a positive and optimistic spirit. Amen.

Daily Prayers

Dear God, help each of us be open to you and follow the direction of your Spirit. May we continue to be instruments of your love, peace, and support. It is in service to each other that we most effectively model our service to you. Regardless of how well our days are going, let us see that you are in the least of our brothers and sisters. As always, we ask for your love, guidance, and support. Amen.

Dear God, help each of us appreciate everything we have. Grant us the serenity to take time each day to think of all the blessings we have been given. May our eyes always be open to see the beauty in nature, may our hearts be open to the power of friendship, and may our souls be open to the gift of faith that moves us. May we live each day as a gift and recognize the opportunities that await us. Amen.

God of friendships, may our life be enriched by the people who dedicate themselves to following you. May the wisdom, faith, and commitment of these people move each of us into a deeper relationship with you. May their words encourage us, their actions inspire us, and their lives enrich us. Amen.

Dear Jesus, grant us the courage and strength to get through the dark days. When failure, sadness, or loneliness weigh us down, stretch out your hand to lift us up. Help us continue to carry our crosses even though we do not understand them. We are encouraged by your example, and know that with you, Lord, all things are possible. Amen.

Dear Jesus, as we deal with the repetition that often marks our days, as well as with disappointments, tensions, and struggles, let us remember you are there with us. Although we bear but a small fraction of the cross you carried, help us carry what we must and do so knowing you walk with us. Amen.

May we always appreciate all that we have, O Lord—our meals, our homes, our friendships, and our faith. May we respect and be grateful to those who provide for us. May our abundant gifts be used to help others know and feel your presence among us. May the respect we have for all your creation lead others to see the awesome love you have for us. We ask all this through Jesus, our brother. Amen.

God of love, we are all called to comfort those who suffer, to reach out to the hungry, to embrace the outcast, and to respond to tragedy. May we always be sensitive to the needs of others and be willing to do what we can to make their lives easier. May our giving be endless and may our joy in this giving bring us peace. We ask this through Jesus, who sacrificed much and gained all. Amen.

Dear Jesus, in the gospel of Matthew (6:24–34) you tell us that we cannot serve two masters: we cannot love both God and money. You tell us not to worry about what we will eat and drink, because God knows about our needs and takes care of them. Instead you tell us to be concerned about the kingdom of God and what it requires of us. Help us, Lord, to listen to your words and not be concerned about tomorrow. May we trust in God, that all will be taken care of. Amen.

Jesus, Prince of peace, bring peace into our homes and our hearts. Teach us to celebrate as you did at the wedding feast in Cana, to be at peace with ourselves as you were in your travels, and to pray to your Father as you did so often. Lord, we celebrate life. We thank you for our families and friends, and for the fruitfulness of your creation. Amen.

Dear God, help each of us make this learning experience a great one. May we appreciate the gift of knowledge and apply ourselves to our studies so that our learning experience is an enriching one. Help teachers and staff teach by word and example, and constantly be aware of their influence on students. May we celebrate the successes of our school community with pride and admiration. May we always be grateful for the opportunity to grow in knowledge and in faith. Amen.

Dear Lord, as we deal with life's discomforts, frustrations, and disappointments, remind us of the strength you demonstrated by carrying your cross. We know that we bear but a small fraction of what you bore. Let us gain strength and comfort from knowing that you journey with us always. Amen.

Ever-present God, Father, Son, and Holy Spirit, we know you are not distant from us; in fact, you dwell within us. We see you in the beauty of nature, in the smile of a child, and in the face of the hungry. May we use all that you have given us—our eyes to see, our hands to work, our hearts to love—in loving service to others. May our acts of kindness and compassion reveal your presence in each of us. Amen.

We give you thanks for our friends, O God of friendship. We pray that we may always choose friends who help nurture the strengths and the gifts that we possess. May we in turn be a source of comfort and strength for our friends. Help us follow the example of Jesus in both the forgiveness we offer our friends as well as the confidence we instill in them. Grant us the discipline to make sacrifices when necessary so that the lives of our friends may be made easier. Amen.

God of gifts, thank you for the blessings you have given us. May we always use our gifts and talents in a way that demonstrates kindness, humility, and compassion. May we continue to do our part in developing our gifts. Keep our hearts and minds open to the direction of the Spirit, who calls us to celebrate our gifts by sharing them with others. Amen.

Dear God, grant each of us a listening heart, so we may lead with wisdom and compassion. Grant each of us an understanding soul, so we may hold our judgment and be willing to forgive. Grant each of us an open mind, so that we may continue to grow in love and service. Amen.

Loving God, help each of us look at our lives and recognize the abundance of blessings we have. May we open our eyes to the world around us and see those who go without food, shelter, and clothing. Help us take a moment to look at the food we have, the homes we live in, and the clothes we wear each day. Grant us a sense of perspective that will move us to sacrifice more in our own lives so we can provide others with the basic necessities. Amen.

We take time today, O God, to say thank you to all those in our community who work so hard to see our talents grow. We thank you for the coaches who spend countless hours in training teams; the teachers who work hard to help us grow in knowledge and develop our talents and abilities; and the staff who facilitate and support the work of the school community. It is through all these people that we are able to grow into the people we have been called to be. And so today, in appreciation of all the teachers, coaches, and staff who work for our benefit, we give thanks to you, O God. Amen.

Dear God, what would life be like if we did not have friends to share our joys with, or to lean on when things get tough? We give thanks to you, O God, for the friends who are our sunshine, for the friends who are always there to offer advice, and willing to listen to the same problem over and over again. We thank you for the friends who are always there, ready to stand up for us if need be. Thank you, God, for all our friends. May you continue to bless them and keep them safe in your love. Amen.

Dear God, in the Book of Proverbs we read, "Do not let loyalty and faithfulness forsake you; bind them around your neck, write them on the tablet of your heart" (3:3). We pray that we always live in the spirit of loyalty and faithfulness. Amen.

Thank you, dear God, for all that you have given us, for the opportunity to learn and share our lives with the people of this school community. When our lives become hectic and stressful, may we be comforted by our faith, our friendships, and our families. When we leave this school, may our memories be of people, of love, of faith. Amen.

Daily Prayers

Today is a new day, loving God, with an opportunity for a fresh start. This day offers us great potential to learn and to grow in your love. This day is ours to have and hold. Let us give this day the best we have, and may our generous giving make it a day to be remembered. Amen.

Gentle God, each of us is created in your image and likeness, yet we are all unique. May we each learn to accept one another and give each other a chance to show who we are and what we are about. It is in giving ourselves time to get to know others, by encouraging them in gentle and supportive ways, that we make wonderful friendships and get to know our friends on a deeper level. We pray that we always be open to meeting new people and forming new friendships. Amen

Just Lord, we know that prejudice is an injustice that no one should suffer. Yet even today prejudicial judgments and treatment continue. May we each do our part to show that judgments about people based on skin color, disabilities, ethnic origin, position, or looks are ill-founded and based on ignorance. By our acts of acceptance, welcome, inclusion, and friendship, may we show others that we are all made equally in the image and likeness of God. May we always be instruments of God's unconditional love and peace. Amen.

God of all, life is filled with many opportunities and possibilities. Every day we face choices, some of which may frighten and scare us. We pray that the Holy Spirit continue to guide and direct us as we make our decisions. May our faith encourage us to spend time in prayer and private reflection so that our choices will be good ones. May our faith give us strength and confidence as we move forward with our decisions, knowing they are rooted in your will for us. Amen.

Loving God, help us demonstrate your love every day. Whether with simple acts or difficult ones, keep us strong and motivated to do good for everyone. Let us continue to work together to accomplish great things, and in so doing be the wind beneath each other's wings. Let us show the world that in simple acts great change can take place. Help us, God, to love and serve each other, as Jesus showed us. Amen.

Dear Jesus, as we continue through this year we pray for the optimism that enables us to face each day with renewed hope and joy. May the promise of the resurrection and your eternal peace enable us to accomplish great things this day. In appreciation of this delicate gift of life may we give all that we have to make this day a bright one for ourselves and for others. Amen.

Dear God, peace of mind is attained in doing what we believe is right. This often involves sacrifice, courage, and belief in oneself. Help each of us learn to recognize the voice of our conscience, to have the faith to follow this voice and in so doing attain peace of mind. Let us never operate out of jealousy, hatred, or self importance. Rather, help us follow Jesus' words: "For those who want to save their life will lose it, and those who lose their life for my sake will find it" (Matthew 16:25). Amen.

Dear Lord, life is filled with many opportunities to make a difference in the world. Help us not get stuck in the mundane routine of the day. Help us see the opportunities that present themselves moment by moment. May our minds work creatively to foster an environment that enables and encourages people to shine. May we be co-creators with you here on earth through all that we do. Amen.

When life's challenges seem too great, we turn to you, O God. We look at the lives of the many saints who have gone before us. May we demonstrate a similar faith and confidence that assists us to overcome our challenges. May we not be discouraged in our struggles but be encouraged by the accomplishments of others who have gone before us. May each of our challenges lead us to greater sensitivity, understanding, and compassion and enable us to be instruments of peace and justice in the lives of others. Amen.

Dear God, help us move beyond ourselves and recognize those who are in need of our help. May we see through the smiles when smiles are a pretense. May we see through the laughter when the laughter is not real. May we see through the assurances when the assurances are shallow. Help us to move beyond our own needs and see those in our midst who reach out to us. May we be perceptive enough to recognize the call for help and strong enough to respond to the call. Amen.

Daily Prayers

May we always feel your presence and your love, God of goodness. As we move through the day may we know that you are there for us and with us, every step of the way. We journey with you always at our side. We know that we can always turn to you and there is never need to hide. You offer forgiveness for all that we have done, and give us love and support. Amen.

Jesus, today we look to your example for setting priorities in our lives. You could have sought power; instead, you lived a humble life. You could have associated with the rich and mighty; instead, you chose to be with the poor and sick. You could have had any material pleasure; instead, you sought to help others find faith. You could have conquered any nation with power and violence; instead, you sought peace and justice. In doing this you asked us to do the same for the least of our brothers and sisters, as we would wish done for ourselves. Let us follow your example, Jesus, and embrace the virtues and values you lived out. Amen.

Loving God, we thank you for all the gifts you have given to us. We thank you for the love you showed in giving us your Son. May we always know that you are there and that we will not be given more than we can handle. Help us turn to you, lean on you, talk to you, and strive to be one with you. Amen.

Dear God, in Scripture we often hear Jesus speak of the kingdom of God. We will never realize the kingdom completely until we are one with Jesus in heaven. However, we can get glimpses of the infinite joy we will experience in the kingdom through our experiences here on earth. One such experience is our friendships. Through friendships we receive a glimpse of the richness we will experience in our relationship with Jesus. Amen.

Dear Lord, we know that we can never truly understand what others face. Help us not judge others or be hard on others. Help us remain sympathetic and kind in all that we say and do. May we never presume that we know someone's pain or anguish. Let us offer only support and guidance to those in our midst who are struggling. Give us the strength to not give up, but to remain strong for those who depend on us. Amen.

Dear Lord, grant each of us the gift of wisdom. May we always have an open heart and do everything with kindness and love. You have chosen us to help build your kingdom here on earth. May we accept this call and respond by exercising prudence, understanding, and love. Amen.

Dear God, we offer ourselves as a living sacrifice to you. We dedicate ourselves to your service and to doing only that which is pleasing to you. This is the true worship we should offer. Do not let us live by the standards of this world, but transform us to be your people. Then we will be able to know your will—what is good and pleasing to you and good for us. Amen.

Dear God, in Scripture we read these words: "Yet even now, says the Lord, return to me with all your heart, with fasting, with weeping, and with mourning; rend your hearts and not your clothing. Return to the Lord, your God, for he is gracious and merciful, slow to anger, and abounding in steadfast love, and relents from punishing" (Joel 2:12–13). Let us return to you, our God, who will enrich our lives with meaning, peace, joy, and love. Amen.

Dear God, we try to live as Paul taught us in Galatians: "My friends, if anyone is detected in a transgression, you who have received the Spirit should restore such a one in a spirit of gentleness. Bear one another's burdens, and in this way you will fulfill the law of Christ. You reap whatever you sow. So let us not grow weary in doing what is right, for we will reap at harvest time, if we do not give up. Whenever we have an opportunity, let us work for the good of all, and especially for those of the family of faith" (Gal 6:1–10). Amen.

Help us give of ourselves each day, O loving God, so that we may make a difference in the lives of others. May our actions and words reflect the gospel message. May we always remain open to serving you through acts of love and compassion, and may those around us come to know and believe in you through our generous acts. May we enable others to see God in all that we say and do. Amen.

Loving God, there will be times when we will be put to the test, when fear and apprehension will try to take control and prevent us from "doing." There will be times when our failures will try to take hold of us and prevent us from moving on. We pray today for the discipline to focus on our inner strength, the infinite reservoir of talents and gifts within, and use these to build your kingdom. Help us see, Lord, that you are always with us. May our fears motivate us to do the impossible and our failures become a source of opportunity and strength. Amen.

Dear God, we pray today for the courage to stand up for what we believe in. May we recognize all that history has taught us and know that we have the power to effect change where change is needed. We ask the Holy Spirit to direct us and the Lord to strengthen us as we review our lives and outline the challenges that lie ahead. Amen.

Creator God, you call us to be servants to all your people. May we have a light heart and a sensitive spirit that will enable us to recognize opportunities to make a difference in someone's life. May we hear your call each day and say "yes" to the invitation to be your followers. Amen.

Dear Jesus, by your life and passion you show that our will and our convictions cannot be taken from us. We all experience many injustices during the course of our lives. May we be granted a courage like yours, that enables us to suffer any accusation, ridicule, or suffering. May we always hold on to that which is important to us and never compromise ourselves because of pressure or embarrassment. Lord, may your example give us the will power we need to always remain true to ourselves and to you. Amen.

Dear Lord, help us accept the difficulties and partings we face in our lives. Grant us the faith and grace to be able to let go of all that we have so that one day we may be at peace with you. Help each of us to be your instruments and continue the great works you began. May we all accept this responsibility in order to build your kingdom here on earth. Amen.

Brittni

Loving God, we pray that we may possess the theological virtues—faith, hope, and charity—in abundance, and that they may direct our actions and our attitude in life. May we be granted the faith to follow the example of Jesus in all that we do. May we be granted hope so that we always have the strength to persevere. May we be granted charity so that we are always willing to give of ourselves to better the lives of others. Amen.

Dear God, we pray that we be blessed with the cardinal virtues—prudence, justice, temperance, and fortitude—so that we may make your Word come alive here on earth. Grant us the prudence to make decisions that embrace and carry out your will. Grant us the desire for justice so that we may work unceasingly at obtaining fairness. Grant us temperance so that we may moderate and pace our actions. Grant us fortitude so that we may endure all that life brings while remaining true to our faith. May these virtues show us the light and the way. Amen.

God of details, life is often busy, filled with expectations and commitments. In this busy schedule may we always be willing to answer Jesus' call to perform the spiritual works of mercy: to counsel the doubtful, instruct the ignorant, admonish the sinner, comfort the sorrowful, forgive injuries, bear wrongs patiently, and pray for the living and the dead. It is in taking time for others, in sharing our gifts and talents, that your love and your presence are made known to the world. May your love inspire us to do all this in your name. Amen.

Dear God, we pray for the gifts of the Holy Spirit: wisdom, understanding, counsel, fortitude, knowledge, piety, and fear of the Lord. May we always feel the presence of the Holy Spirit directing us and guiding us. May we use the gifts that the Spirit offers to help others who struggle with decisions in their own lives. May we do all this in love and service to you, O Lord. Amen.

Dear God, we pray for the fruits of the Holy Spirit: love, joy, peace, patience, kindness, goodness, faithfulness, gentleness, and self-control. We know that these fruits are life's greatest blessings. May we use these blessings to help others find faith in your Word. Amen.

CHAPTER TWO

Prayers for the Liturgical Seasons

Advent

First Week of Advent

Theme: Anticipation and longing for the coming of Jesus

Light the first candle on your Advent wreath, if you are using one.

All powerful and loving God, increase our strength of will to do good so that we can each be instruments of your love here on earth. May we prepare for Christmas and the coming of Jesus with an open mind and heart and thus allow this Christmas to have special meaning for each of us. May your love for each of us bring us ever closer to you. Amen.

Other prayers for the first week of Advent:

All powerful and loving God, help each of us to feel your love for us. May our celebration of the birth of Jesus be a time of great joy. May we come to know the depths of your love in our search to get to know you more intimately. Give us a generous heart so we may spread this love throughout the world by sharing your love with all people. Amen.

Jesus, you are the light of the world. Help each of us to leave the darkness behind and to live in your light. As we prepare for the celebration of your birth may we recall your wondrous ways. Make us thoughtful and generous so that we can celebrate your birth in the light of true joy and gladness. Amen.

Jesus, you are our brother and our friend. You showed us how to live life in a meaningful way. You reached out to the poor, you comforted the outcasts, you healed the sick, and you treated each person with dignity and respect. As we prepare to celebrate your birth, help us show the effect you have had on each of our lives by following your example and the life that you lived. Amen.

God of love and life, as we prepare for Christmas help each of us to take time during the day to talk to you. Because we long to celebrate the birth of Jesus, may we make an effort to think each day of how wonderful an event his birth was. Help us reflect on your invitation to love and follow you. May the birth of Jesus draw us closer to you and your Son. Amen.

Second Week of Advent
Theme: Preparation for the coming of Jesus

Light the first and second candles on your Advent wreath, if you are using one.

Dear God, as we draw closer to the celebration of the birth of Jesus Christ, help each of us grow in faith and in love. During our journey through this Advent season, help us take moments throughout the day and think about the impact Jesus' coming had on our world. Help us open our heart to your light, and let this light shine in our own lives and the lives of those we meet. Amen.

Other prayers for the second week of Advent:

God of hope, help each of us take time from our busy schedule and prepare for the celebration of Jesus' birth. Through the life of Jesus and the fulfillment of his mission may we gain the promise of salvation. Let the joy that this brings to our hearts keep our faith alive and make us desirous of going out and making disciples of all the nations. Amen.

Dear Lord, as we prepare for the celebration of your birth give each of us the strength to love you more dearly. Your life changed history forever. We know of the love that God has for us and the forgiveness that we are offered for our weakness and failings. May this love and forgiveness allow us to be sensitive and compassionate with all those we deal with, especially during this Advent season. Amen.

Loving God, may the love that you showed us in the birth of your Son help each of us offer aid to others who could benefit from our gifts. May this season be one where we go beyond our own wants and think of others in our community and in the world who need our care. Amen.

Third Week of Advent
Theme: Rejoicing in anticipation of Christmas

Light the first, second, and third candles on your Advent wreath, if you are using one.

Lord God, we rejoice at the birth of your Son, Jesus. We listen to the words of John the Baptist who says: "There is one more powerful than I coming after me. I am not worthy to carry his sandals." This reference to the coming of Jesus shows his great power and love. We rejoice in the care and embrace of a loving God who continuously invites us to follow his Son. In preparation of the birth of Jesus, may we say yes to this invitation. Amen.

Other prayers for the third week of Advent:

God of joy, we pray for all those who are filled with sadness and confusion, that they may be touched by the joy of the Christmas season. May each of us be instruments who bring this joy to them. In their search for self-confidence, direction, and reassurance, may they find comfort and light in God. Amen.

Dear God, help each of us to remain humble and faith-filled people. We only need to look at the example of Jesus to see what humility and compassion mean. Help us imitate these and other virtues that Jesus showed us how to practice. May this Christmas be a season where we learn to adopt gospel values and live faith-filled lives. Amen.

Prayers for the Liturgical Seasons

May each of us experience great joy this Advent season, O Lord. As we prepare for Christmas, may we never lose sight of what this season is all about; the birth of our savior who calls each of us to the joy of eternal life. May our faith enable us to embrace this joy on earth and live out all that Jesus has called us to. Amen.

God of the ages, Christmas is often an exciting time. Help us to experience the true joy of the season. We buy gifts for family and friends who occupy a special place in our heart. May we appreciate them more and more. May we remember those who do not have such blessings and spend time making this season one of joy for them. Amen.

Lord of all, as we draw closer to the birth of Jesus may we spend time thinking of those who do not feel the joy of the season. We pray today for all those who are suffering, physically or emotionally, and pray that they may find peace. May we take concrete action to bring joy to these people and in so doing share the spirit this season offers. Amen.

Fourth Week of Advent

Theme: God's love and hope

Light all four candles on your Advent wreath, if you are using one.

As we approach Christmas, dear God, help each of us recognize what Jesus has done for us and the new direction he has given us. May each of us this Christmas make a special effort to live out Jesus' example and make this Christmas a beautiful one. Amen.

Other prayers for the fourth week of Advent:

God of love, you made us a new creation through Jesus. May his coming free us from sin and renew your life within us and within all people on earth. Amen.

Loving God, as we draw closer to the celebration of the birth of Jesus Christ, help each of us grow in faith and in love. May we open our hearts to his light, and let this light shine in the lives of others. May this Christmas have real meaning for each of us as we find ways of helping one another. Amen.

God of love, as we approach Christmas day, may we all feel the true spirit of Christmas, a spirit that tells us of God's great love for each of us. May we appreciate the meaning of the birth of Christ, a birth that has changed history forever. His birth allows each of us to be more fully alive, knowing that Jesus' birth offers us salvation and love. May this Christmas bring joy and peace. Amen.

God of love, fill each of us with the joy of the Christmas spirit, and share it with others by comforting the lonely, seeking friendship with the outcast, feeding the hungry, and defending the weak. May each of us work this Christmas toward developing the wonderful virtues that Jesus showed us, may we treat each person with dignity and help them have the courage to be who they are. May each of us be instruments of God's love. We ask this through Jesus our brother and Savior. Amen.

God of joy, we look forward to the celebration of the birth of Jesus. May your love inspire us to take extra time to deepen our relationship with you. During this Christmas season may we become faith-filled people who help spread the gospel in all that we say and do. May the comfort of your presence in our lives lighten our hearts and bring us great joy and peace. Amen.

Feast of the Holy Family

The feast of the Holy Family causes us to pause and look at Jesus' family. We see that they too went through struggles, hardships, and suffering. Today we give thanks for our families and look at how we can become closer and more united. We know that there will always be difficult times, times where we do not agree, times when we take our anger out on each other, times when we simply want time by ourselves. What we recognize during all of these times is that family is a source of love, strength, and comfort. We pray today that our families will always be a place we can seek refuge and love.

Prayers for the Liturgical Seasons

Loving God, help each of us who are members of a family to be understanding, compassionate, and considerate with one another. May we let other family members know that we will always be there for them, no matter what the problem, issue, or trouble. Help us stand in the other person's shoes so that we can be more sympathetic to the issues and pressures that others in our family face. May our family provide a place of comfort, a place that models the unconditional love Jesus showed us. And may our families be filled with peace and happiness. Amen.

Feast of the Epiphany (First Sunday of the New Year)

At the liturgy on the feast of the Epiphany, we hear the story of the three wise men who visited the baby Jesus, bringing him gifts. The Christmas story is all about gift giving. The wonderful gift of Jesus that God gives to the world and the wonderful gifts that we give back.

This time of the year is a time of resolutions. If you have not made your new year's resolution yet, here is something for you to consider: spend time thinking of all the wonderful things you did for others during this past year. These actions are a reflection of who you are. Reflect on these, then make your new year's resolution to continue to give back to God the gift of yourself, to give back to God through helping others.

Dear God, help us see more clearly the gift we are to the world and the potential we have within us. Help us share this with the world. We ask this through Jesus your Son. Amen.

Lent

During Lent we ask ourselves more directly: "What is it that God asks of us?" We find the answer throughout the gospels. We listen closely to the words of Jesus who says: "Whoever wants to be first must place himself last and be servant of all."

Reflection and prayer for the Monday before Ash Wednesday

This Wednesday we will begin the holy season of Lent. We can begin to prepare ourselves for Lent throughout this week by thinking of the kind of choices and sacrifices we want to make to renew our relationship with God. We are always challenged to make this relationship stronger. Whatever we do, we want to stay in God's presence. Lent is a time to exercise discipline in our lives, to live in such a way that brings us closer to God. This faithfulness is practiced not just in acts of charity and fasting; it is also shown in the choices we make every moment. The question we should ask is whether what we are doing at this moment is pleasing to God.

Lord, I desire to do all things for your glory. I do not wish to do things for my own self-interest or to satisfy my ego. I desire to do all things in your name, for your cause, for your mission. Give me the strength, Lord, to live in a manner worthy of my relationship with you. Give me the strength to live a disciplined life so that all that I do is for your glory. Then I will know peace in my heart. Amen.

Reflection and prayer for the Tuesday before Ash Wednesday

Tomorrow is Ash Wednesday; it is the beginning of Lent. On that day we abstain from meat and eat less. We pray that this lenten journey will enable us to leave our sins in the dust and work at revealing God's love.

During this season of Lent let us think about the love you have for us, O Lord, in giving us your only Son, who died in order to save us. It is this love that acts as an invitation for all of us to turn to you, and to renew and strengthen our relationship with you. May this bring great meaning to this lenten season for each of us. Amen.

Alternate reflection and prayer for the Tuesday before Ash Wednesday

Today is what some refer to as Shrove Tuesday (Mardi Gras). This is French for "Fat Tuesday." In medieval times, the period between the Epiphany and Lent was generally a time of great festivity. This culminated on the eve of Lent in a carnival atmosphere. Since the time of fasting was about to begin, the forbidden foods had to be used up so they didn't spoil. Tomorrow is Ash Wednesday, a day on which we abstain from meat and begin our lenten journey. We pray today that this journey will bring each of us closer to God.

Good and gracious God, as we prepare for Lent, help us come to know the love you have for each one of us. You accepted the death of your Son for our salvation. Help each of us take time in the season of Lent to be with you, in prayer and in moments of silence. May our hearts and minds be filled with the wonder of all that you have offered us, and may we in turn respond with acceptance and love. We ask all this through Christ our Lord. Amen.

Ash Wednesday

Today is Ash Wednesday, the beginning of our lenten journey.

Dear God, as we enter this season of Lent help each of us be willing to give of ourselves so we can make the lives of others easier. May our actions and words reflect the gospel message. May we always remain open to serving you through acts of love and compassion. May those around us come to know and believe in you through our own generous acts of giving and kindness. We ask this through Jesus our Lord and Savior. Amen.

Alternate prayer for Ash Wednesday

Loving God, as we begin our lenten journey help each of us grow in our relationship with you. May our acts of self-giving and sacrifice lead us to empty ourselves and welcome you into our hearts, minds and souls. May the sacrifice of your Son and the depths of your love fill our hearts with joy, and may we make this joy known to all those with whom we live and work. Amen.

Lenten prayers

Saving God, we know that it is in and through Jesus' death that we have the promise of eternal life. It is in his words and works that your love and the love of your Son for us is made known. It is a love so great that we want to respond by saying yes to Jesus. It is a love so great that it affects who we are, and how we live. It is a love so great that we recognize the gift of eternal life as a gift beyond measure. May each of us live by saying yes to your love for us in the hope of one day being united with you. Amen .

Lord of all, help us continue to be a source of strength and support for one another. We never know the pain and suffering that those around us bear. We look at smiles that often hide great sorrow. We look at faces that display no pain. May we always provide comfort to those around us, exercise patience in times of trial, and offer a place of refuge for those whose suffering is too great to bear. Amen.

Loving Father, the love that Jesus has for each of us was evident in his life and in the sacrifice of himself. Help each of us in our struggles to accept our suffering as Jesus did, and to work toward healing with knowledge of the love that Jesus has for us. May we be a source of comfort and strength for each other as we help each other carry our crosses. Amen.

Dear Lord, we strive to do your will. We don't follow the goals of this world because people often make material gain or power their goals. We choose your path, a path that is worthwhile, a path of love and service. In this way, all that we do is good, all that comes from what we do will be good. Amen.

Loving God, you call us to be servants to all your people. Through our acts of faith may we bring others to you. Send your Spirit so that we may have the gift of humility, to extinguish selfish desires, to see that all people are one family, and to carry out your message to feed the hungry and comfort those who suffer. We seek to do all things to glorify you, Lord, and to grow in union with you. Amen.

Holy Week

During this Holy Week we remember God's love for us and look forward to the celebration of the resurrection of Jesus. "Be joyful always, pray continuously, give thanks in all circumstances, for this is God's will for you in Christ."

As we continue to journey through this season of Lent we remember the great sacrifice that Jesus made for each of us. He offered himself to show his love for us, so that we could be people of joy, knowing that we have the promise of eternal life. For this we give great thanks to God and prepare for the celebration of Jesus' resurrection. Amen.

Healing God, stretch out your hand and heal us. Shine your light on the darkness of accusations and pessimism. We crave the goodness of your light; we desire freedom from distractions and sin. Just as you brought Lazarus back to life, may your word bring us new life. Amen.

Dear God, in your plan of salvation your Son, Jesus, accepted the cross and freed us from sin. May we accept our crosses and help one another carry them. May our actions show love for our neighbor and love for God. May we come to share in the glory of Jesus' resurrection. Amen.

Father, by the Easter mystery you touch our lives with the healing power of your love. You have given us freedom and the promise of eternal life. May we who celebrate your gift, find joy in it forever in heaven. May each of us make your love known in all that we say and do. May we share with others the sense of hope that you have given to us. We ask all this through Jesus our Savior. Amen.

Holy Thursday

The day before Jesus died, he gathered his disciples to celebrate the Passover Seder. He wanted to encourage them before his coming death and institute the eucharistic meal we celebrate over 2000 years later. Let us remember, as we approach this Easter, that Jesus gave his life for our salvation.

Dear God, help each of us to look upon the example of Christ as a model for our actions. May we reach out to others as Jesus did with great faith and humility. Just as it was not beneath Jesus to wash the feet of his disciples, let each of us be able to help one another by simple gestures. Let the celebration and joy of the Resurrection touch each of us this Easter, and help us live by the example Christ set for us. Amen.

Easter

Alleluia! We celebrate with great joy, O God, the resurrection of our Lord and Savior, Jesus Christ. We think of the great happiness and excitement that was experienced at the news of the rising of Jesus. All that was promised came true in and through his resurrection. All his people were now able to feel great joy even though they knew of his suffering and death. Help us to carry the joy of this season with us each and every day of the year. Alleluia!

Father, by the Easter mystery you touch our lives with the healing power of your love. You have given us the freedom and the promise of eternal life. May we who celebrate your gift, find joy in it forever in heaven. May each of us make your love known in all that we say and do. May we instill in others the sense of hope that you have given to us. We ask all this through Jesus our Savior. Amen.

Pentecost

Pentecost coincided with the great annual festival that the Jewish people celebrated. This was a celebration of the harvest and the reception of the Torah on Mount Sinai. It was on this day that a great event took place. Through the outburst of the Holy Spirit, which came both as the sound of wind and the visible sign of tongues of fire, the disciples gained great confidence and courage. They spoke in languages that they had no prior knowledge of. Those who witnessed this event were amazed. We do not often receive such strong visible signs of the presence of the Holy Spirit. However we know that the Spirit dwells within us, enabling us to do great things.

Spirit of God, may we, as your followers, feel the courage and faith that the disciples felt at Pentecost. May we too become heralds of your gospel; speaking and living unceasingly the message that Jesus gave us on earth. May our minds and hearts always be open to you and may our words and actions help to transform people of all nations. Amen.

Feast of the Holy Trinity

God the Father, God the Son, and God the Holy Spirit. Trinity Sunday celebrates the mystery of the Trinity, three Persons in one God. These three Persons dwell in us and offer us love and hope.

Dear God, we pray today that we come to know you more intimately, God, Father, Son, and Holy Spirit. May we know your love for us. God the Father, you sent us your Son so that we may be saved. Through the mission and message Jesus delivered on earth we learn how to treat one another. We have learned of the promise of our own salvation. May we remain open to you, God the Spirit, who is there always to guide and direct us. We only need the faith and confidence to listen to your voice, which is always there to guide and direct us. May we embrace the threefold mystery persons of the Trinity and may they assist us in our daily living. Amen.

Feast of the Body and Blood of Christ

In the celebration of the Eucharist, we, as Catholics, are invited to share in the body and blood of Christ. We take and eat Jesus' body and drink his blood. This provides us with nourishment for our lives.

Dear God, Jesus said to us: "I am the living bread who has come down from heaven. Whoever eats of this bread will live forever; and the bread I will give for the life of the world is my flesh"(John 6:51). Help each of us to experience the presence of Jesus within us. May Jesus' presence lead us daily into living faith-filled lives. When others look at us may they see Jesus within us. May our example help to transform the world. Amen.

Feast of the Sacred Heart of Jesus

We know the love that dwells in the heart of Jesus, a love that reaches out to people of all time.

Jesus, you taught us to see each and every person as a child of God. You encourage us to take the time and help one person who is struggling, because that person is worthy of our attention and time. Your love for each of us is so great that if we think about it we shall be moved to tears. Help us share this love that you have for us with one another. Help us put aside judgments, prejudice, and anger. May we live out the love you have blessed us with. Help us make decisions in life that foster this love, and may we grow in this love daily. Amen.

Feast of the Immaculate Heart of Mary

We look to the heart of Mary and see great faith and love. We know of the love that she had for Jesus; we see part of the power of that love in a mother's love for her child. We can only imagine what the world would be like if it was filled with the love and the faith that Mary possessed. We pray to Mary today that through her prayers we may more easily live a life of love.

Dear Mary, our Mother, there are times in our lives where we get upset and do not understand events, actions, or decisions made by others. We look at your experience with Jesus when, at the age of twelve, he stayed behind in Jerusalem after the celebration of the Passover. You were worried and did not understand why Jesus would do this and upset you. However, when Jesus answered, you knew that it was the will of God. Your faith and trust in God enabled you to better accept Jesus' action. We pray that through your prayers we, too, will be given a deep love and faith commitment. May we accept things in life that we do not understand. We pray today that, through your intercession, we continue to grow in love and faith daily. Amen.

Christ the King (Last Sunday of Ordinary Time)

Since Jesus walked the earth there has been an endless number of books written about him, many attempting to understand him, interpreting his works and life. A person could spend a lifetime studying the Scriptures and writing about the life and times of Jesus. The reading for the feast of Christ the King is a great summary of what Jesus was all about (Year A - Matthew 25:31–46; Year B - John 18:33–37; Year C - Luke 23:35–43). They are the readings we should reflect on if we want to truly understand the mission and message of Jesus and what he expects of us. It is from these readings that we arrive at the corporal works of mercy. Our prayer today is part of this reading.

Let us pray… Jesus will say to the people on his right "come you that are blessed by my Father, inherit the kingdom prepared for you from the foundation of the world. For I was hungry and you gave me food, I was thirsty and you gave me something to drink, I was a stranger and you welcomed me, naked and you gave me clothing, I was sick and you took care of me, I was in prison and you visited me… Just as you did it to one of the least of these who are members of my family, you did it to me." Amen.

CHAPTER THREE

Thematic Prayers for the School Year

New Semester or New School Year

Loving God, we pray for your blessing upon each of us. May we approach the beginning of the school year as a new start. Help us form friendships with those who enable us to become better persons. Friendships will enable each and everyone one of us to shine. Help us develop our faith so that we possess courage and confidence to develop the gifts we have been blessed with. Help us be compassionate and loving people so the world may know your love and healing power, O God. May this year be one of great peace and happiness for us and our families. Amen.

God of life, may this school year be filled with academic and spiritual growth. May we each be willing to help others. Help us come to know Jesus better and follow the example of love that he shared. Give us the strength and faith to make his love known here on earth. Amen.

As we begin this school year, O Lord, may we make the right choices so we will learn better. May we listen to the voice of the Holy Spirit, which is a powerful guide in all the decisions we make. We ask this through Jesus our Lord and Savior. Amen.

Dear God, beginnings are not always easy. Changes are difficult for many of us. We perform to the best of our ability when we feel comfortable and relaxed, so we pray today for the sense of calm and comfort that your love brings. May each of us feel this comfort in our hearts. Help us share the wonderful gifts you have blessed us with. Amen.

Good and gracious God, we know that with faith and trust in you all things are possible. During this new beginning help us each feel your presence and your calming influence in our lives. May the knowledge and awareness of your power assist each of us as we learn during this year. Amen.

Dear God, you have blessed us with friendships. Help each of us be open to meeting and making new friends as we begin this school year. Give us the wisdom to tell which friends will be there to help us no matter what difficulties we face. Bless these friends and keep them close to us always. Amen.

Loving God, help us begin this school year with a renewed spirit of love and faith. When life's challenges seem to overwhelm us, may we rely on your friendship and love. When our studies cause pressure and stress, may we feel the sense of calm that faith brings. When we let faith work in our lives, everything falls into place. Life is filled with peace and everything takes on fuller meaning. Amen.

God of all creation, as we begin this year we pray it may be filled with great spirit, fun, excitement, and of course enjoyable and meaningful learning. We know that the year depends in great measure on what we give, so let us give as much as we can to make this year a wonderful one. Amen.

As we begin this year, O Lord, give us the confidence to be ourselves and share our gifts. We ask for the guidance of the Holy Spirit as we meet new people. May we find and form friendships that help us develop all our gifts. May we feel comfortable in being ourselves and be blessed with friends who accept us as we are. Give us the courage to live out our faith in our studies and our extracurricular and personal lives. Grant us peace in who we are and joy in all we do. Amen.

As we begin this semester/year, dear God, help each of us look at this beginning as an opportunity to "go the extra mile." This semester will offer many occasions to contribute to this community. We ask for the desire and strength to do all we can and to be there for each other, so that this semester is a fantastic one. Amen.

Let this semester/year be filled with a sharing of our gifts. O God of love, let the simple gestures we perform be filled with love. May we recognize all that we are, and work to do our best. In all this may we feel your presence, in life's every test. We know through experience that life's not easy. However, we have our family, friends, and faith to strengthen us in our pain. It is in living out your love, O God, that life gains its greatest meaning. So this year we are ready for friends to lean on us. Give us love and let us know we can do all this with your grace, O God and Father of all. Amen.

God of light, as we begin this semester/year, may we be a source of light for those around us. May we comfort those who are upset, reach out to those who are struggling, love those who feel they are unlovable, and defend those who are too weak to defend themselves. In doing this may we help others shine and allow them to use the gifts you have blessed them with. May our actions be a source of light and hope for all our brothers and sisters. Amen.

Lord of wisdom, as we begin this semester/year we already face many decisions. May we make choices that will assist us in using all our gifts. We pray for the strength to face the difficult challenges and obstacles that present themselves. May we not only look to the immediate future, but also consider the long-term effect and impact of our decisions. Give us the comfort of supportive and loyal friends. Finally, may we always listen to the voice of the Spirit in our hearts. Amen.

Parent/Teacher Interviews

Today our parents have the opportunity to meet our teachers. We pray that these meetings may be fruitful and lead to our future growth and development both spiritually and academically.

L oving God, as our progress is discussed between our teachers and parents, help each of us to profit from this time. May we see our school experience as a time to discover, nurture, and develop our gifts. May our faith give us the confidence that replaces stress with peace. May our teachers give us the knowledge that replaces questions with answers. May our friends give us the support that replaces fear with courage. We pray in a special way for our teachers. At this busy time give them the strength to carry out their duties. May our parents be understanding and accepting as they continue to guide us through the hard times. Amen.

For Grade Eight Students (Orientation)

D ear God, we pray today for all our grade eight student visitors. May they feel welcome into our community. May they feel comfortable enough to express their true selves, realizing that we are all made in the image and likeness of God. We recognize that there is some fear and trepidation entering into high school—a new environment, a new beginning. May all our grade eight guests recognize these feelings as normal. Help them, God, to discover and develop their gifts. May they do this by recognizing these gifts are from you, and the perfect way to say "thank you, God" is to use their gifts to benefit and help others. Amen.

D ear God, this afternoon we welcome grade eight students to this community. We pray for a special blessing on these students, that each of them is able to discover the gifts that you have blessed them with. May they use these gifts for the benefit of others in loving service to you. Amen.

For Grade Nine Students

As we begin our first year of high school we pray that our high school years be filled with wonderful achievements.

Dear God, as we begin this experience, help us feel comfortable and relaxed in this new environment. We know we are here to receive a good education. We will learn both academically as well as spiritually. During our journey, may we have the confidence to share all our gifts and the courage and strength to live out who we truly are. Amen.

For Grade Ten Students

As we enter our second year of high school we feel a little more comfortable. We pray that this comfort provide us with encouragement to follow our dreams and accomplish them.

Dear God, we pray that we never underestimate our capabilities. May we never hold back from seeking our dreams and making them a reality. We pray for the faith, confidence, strength and determination to set our sights high and to achieve all that we dream of. May the next three years be filled with wonderful accomplishments and successes. May we do this together, as a community and as a family. Amen.

For Grade Eleven Students

As we enter our third year of high school we pray for the insight and energy to make these last years successful.

Dear God, during this important year may we be constantly encouraged to do the best we can. As we feel more comfortable and confident as grade eleven students, help us to develop and nurture our own gifts. May we have the courage to stand up for what we believe in, and the compassion to reach out and help others. Give us the faith to be open to the voice of the Spirit. We pray that this year be filled with our greatest blessings and that we enjoy and share them, together as a community and as a family. Amen.

For Grade Twelve Students

As we enter our last year of high school we strive to make this a year filled with success.

Dear God, as we face this last year of high school, bless each of us with strength and enthusiasm. May we tackle this year with energy and a strong commitment to succeed. May we each do our personal best, giving all we can give. Finally, we pray for the guidance of the Holy Spirit. May all our decisions be well thought out, filled with good counsel, and open to the Spirit. Amen.

For Our Secretaries

Dear God, we thank you for our secretaries. Please grant them a special blessing today. May their lives be filled with joy and their hearts with peace. Let each of us appreciate all that they do for us and take time to extend gestures of appreciation in return. May they always see the importance of what they do and may this be revealed in the thanks that we as a community extend to them. Loving God, help them recognize their call to carry out your mission in their every act and gesture. Let their good work be a living example to all of us of how to build your kingdom here on earth. Amen.

For Staff Meetings

We call upon you, Lord, to send the gifts of your Spirit. We ask that you enlighten all of us as leaders with the gifts of wisdom, prudence, fortitude, and compassion, so we can be a true light to those we work with and the students we serve. Working together as a spiritual family for the purpose of your kingdom, we ask you, Lord, for the courage to always do your will, the spirit of understanding to appreciate each other's gifts, and the strength to help each other endure through the difficult times. Amen.

Lord God, we pray that as spiritual leaders of this community, we may continue to develop and nurture the gifts we have been blessed with. As we make decisions, may we always be open to the Spirit enabling God to work in and through us. May our example, our dedication, and our compassion comfort and inspire those we lead. Amen.

Dear God, help each of us empower our youth by encouraging and supporting them. May they develop and fulfill all of their gifts with confidence and courage. May they accept the responsibility that is theirs, for it is in this acceptance that they shine and their true potential is revealed. May our youth be blessed with prudence, respond to the call to justice, and forever remain open to the Holy Spirit. Amen.

For Ourselves as Teachers

Dear God, you have called us to be teachers. As pressures become burdensome, help us never lose sight of our mission. May your love provide us with the comfort and confidence we need to meet all of life's challenges. May our own faith life be an inspiration to all those with whom we live and work. Amen.

Student Appreciation

Dear God, we thank you for the wonderful students we have here in our school. May we help them learn to recognize the gifts they possess and to never underestimate their potential. May we give them the confidence and knowledge they need to achieve their dreams. Amen.

God of all, we give thanks today for all our students and the contributions they have made to this community. May they be blessed for all that they do. May they be encouraged to continue to share their gifts and talents. Let them be supported as they risk, as they give, and as they grow. Amen.

Teacher Appreciation

Jesus, divine Teacher, you have blessed us with many wonderful people in our lives. Today we thank you for our teachers. We thank you not only for what they teach, but more importantly, how they teach. We thank you for their care, concern, guidance, and love; for their academic contributions and extracurricular contributions. In appreciation for all they do for us, that affect so many areas of our lives, we their students give thanks today. We ask you, Jesus, to bless our teachers. May they know that their example of faith and concern has tremendous impact on our lives. Grant them peace and strength, now and always. Amen.

God of knowledge, today we pray for our teachers. In the words of Jean Vanier, founder of the L'Arche community: "Teachers are like gardeners. They provide us with all the things we need to grow: knowledge, wisdom, advice, comfort, support and love, enabling us to develop to our full potential. In and through this delicate act of gardening, of caring and giving, the teacher facilitates the beautiful development of the life within the seed." Thank you, God, for blessing us with such beautiful gardeners. Amen.

Thematic Prayers for the School Year

Thanksgiving

Good and gracious God, this time of year we think of all the things we should be thankful for. We take a moment today to give thanks for the blessings you have given us. Thank you for our friends, our families, for laughter, for sunshine, for the gentle rains, and the beautiful skies. May we always see the blessings in our lives and take time to appreciate them. Amen.

Dear Jesus, thank you for all the blessings and the treasures you have showered upon us. Thank you for family, friends, knowledge, wisdom, and all your angels and saints who guide us in our journey of building up your kingdom. We ask you, Lord Jesus, to bless our gifts, bless our lives, and bless this day. Amen.

Thank you, God of love, for the many gifts you have given us. Help each of us take time to recognize the gifts you have given us and work toward developing those gifts. May we be willing to reach out to others and share our blessings. Amen.

Thank you for the gift of life, O Lord—for the joy of seeing your magnificent work of nature, the chance to see flowers grow and leaves change colors. Thank you for wonderful people, family members, and friends whom we spend time with. Thank you for the time you give us to laugh, to play sports, to be part of a club. Thank you for the gift of life. Amen.

Thank you for the gifts of discipline and knowledge, O Lord. May we never underestimate our potential and may we follow our dreams to achieve greatness. As we grow, let us always keep in mind that holiness is the only true greatness. May we always work to help others. May we show compassion and concern for all those around us, and share our knowledge in a way that transforms the world. Amen.

God of all gifts, we give you thanks for the many blessings you have given us. May we always appreciate everything: our meals, our home, our friendships, and our faith. May we respect both the people who provide for us as well as the love and dedication you offer. May the abundance of our gifts be used to assist others to know you and feel your presence among us. May others see in creation the awesome love that you have for us. We ask all this through Christ our Lord. Amen.

Loving God, we thank you for the many gifts you have given to us. In the midst of our busy days help us see the beauty that surrounds us. May your creation cause us to pause, to open our eyes and hearts wider. May we know and feel the great love you have for us and the tremendous power you offer us. Amen.

Dear God, we take time today to acknowledge all those people in our lives who live out their Christian witness and by so doing make our lives easier. For those who go out of their way to comfort us when we are down, for those who spend time with us when we are overwhelmed and in need of help, for those who are simply there, quietly offering their love through their presence. For all these individuals in our lives we pray and give thanks to you God. May each of us every day be aware of the support and love these people show us. May we actively return their love. Amen.

Exams

This week we begin taking exams. We know that this is a stressful and difficult time for many. We remember that what is most important is that we each dedicate ourselves to our studies and do the best that we can. This is all God asks of us, and it is all that we can ask of ourselves. We pray today a special spiritual blessing taken from St. Paul's letter to the Ephesians.

Let us give thanks to God for in our union with Christ he has blessed us by giving us every spiritual blessing in the heavenly world. Even before the world was made, God had already chosen us to be God's through our union with Christ. Let us praise God for God's glorious grace, for the free gift God gave us in Jesus, for by the sacrificial death of Christ we are set free, our sins are forgiven. How great is the grace of God. Amen. (Eph 1:3–14)

Thematic Prayers for the School Year

Student's prayer to St. Joseph of Cupertino

O St. Joseph of Cupertino, who while on earth asked God's help with your examinations, obtain for us a like favor in the examinations for which we are preparing. Amen.

God of knowledge, as these days pass and students prepare for exams, we pray for peace of mind. Many students face decisions that will affect the rest of their lives, so we pray for prudence. When students feel the pressure of the final stretch, we pray for a sense of calm. As teachers we work very hard to complete courses and mark assignments and tests. Please give us patience and strength. May each of us feel the presence and love of God as we proceed through these days. Amen.

Dear God, thank you for the ability to learn and share our lives with beautiful people. In this hectic and stressful time may we be comforted by our faith, our friendships, and our families. May the significance and priority of these things in our life bring comfort, for we know when all this is over, our memories will be of people, of love, and of faith. Amen.

God, help us stay calm as we write this exam. We know you are present, and your presence can provide us with peace and comfort. May we write all that we know and have studied. If we become stressed, help us relax and sort out our confusion. If we need to guess, we pray the guess is a good one! Amen.

As we continue to study and prepare for exams, O God, may we remember you are with us: in math as we work through our calculations; in science as we discover our formulas; in English as we draft our essays; in religion as we grow in faith; in geography as we learn about the world around us; in all the subjects we study. Thank you for guiding us and giving us your light. Amen.

Dear God, as we approach the last week of classes, we pray for a sense of calm in the hectic and pressured pace. May we remain focused to do the best we can. May we be able to work hard so that all we have learned will be reflected in our exams. May we always appreciate those who have taught us and the privilege of receiving a great education. Amen.

Graduation

Loving God, as our graduates come together this week to celebrate their graduation from high school may they feel the joy that this accomplishment brings. As they make decisions about which roads to take, may they always have the support of friends and family. When they feel moments of doubt and hesitation, may we, as their schoolmates, friends, and teachers, provide an ear to listen and offer encouragement that gives them strength. May their future be filled with great happiness and faith. We ask all this through Jesus our Lord and Savior. Amen.

Lord God, we pray today for our graduates. May they recognize the contributions they have made to this community. Help them recognize their gifts as they make decisions about their future. May they be guided and supported on their journey by their family, friends, teachers, and staff of this community. Bless them with a healthy, happy, and rewarding future, in which they clearly see their ability and never cease to follow their dreams. Amen.

We celebrate the academic success of our graduates, and recognize the contributions of all the teachers, assistants, administrators, secretaries, caretakers, and support staff who assist all of us, as together we take another step toward the future.

We thank you, O Lord, for all the people in our lives who help us attain our goals. We give thanks for those who offer us comfort when we are down, encouragement in times of defeat; compassion in times of trial, knowledge in times of doubt, and love at all times. May we truly support one another and model the example of our brother and friend, Jesus. Amen.

As a community we celebrate today the graduation of a number of our students. Thank you, loving God, for blessing us with our fantastic teachers, who have worked hard to assist these young men and women in their journey. We also thank you for all the staff who worked so hard to make this day an enjoyable one for these grads. As these teachers and staff members share their gifts for the benefit of students, we pray that the students graduating will also share their gifts with the world. May they have the confidence and strength to fulfill their dreams and the direction and support to overcome life's challenges. We ask all this through our Lord and Savior Jesus Christ. Amen.

Grace for a Graduation Dinner

We come together to celebrate the achievement of graduating from high school. It is a day of great joy and excitement. We reflect on the numerous and varied contributions that we have made throughout our high school experience. We thank God for the ability he has given us and for the support and comfort we have given to and received from one another. With these thoughts in mind we pray:

God of love and life, we thank you for the wonderful gifts you have given each of us. We are grateful for the ability to share these gifts for the benefit of each other. Bless each of us here tonight as well as the grads and staff who are unable to be here with us. As we go our separate ways, may we cherish the sense of identity we have gained through our entire high school experience. We thank you for the food we are about to share and ask you to bless it. In Jesus' name. Amen.

We come together this evening, O Lord, after a busy few days, to celebrate our academic achievements and wonderful blessings. We take a moment to think, not of our hurts and problems, but to focus on all the good things in our lives, particularly the friendships, laughs, and special moments of the past four years. Thank you, God, for these memories. May they remain with us and inspire us always. In celebration, we now share in this special meal, for which we are grateful. We ask you, God, to bless this food and bless each and every one of us. Amen.

Prayer Services in the Event of Death

Two different services are offered below. Each consists of opening remarks, opening prayer, Scripture reading/poem, concluding prayer.

Death of a Student

Death is never easy. It is particularly difficult when a young person dies unexpectedly. We experience great sorrow, pain, confusion, and anger. It is with all of these feelings that we turn to our loving and merciful God and ask that God embrace _____ and grant him/her eternal peace and happiness. We also ask that all family and friends be granted the strength to deal with this tragedy and find comfort in one another and in faith. With this in mind, we pray: (go to the opening prayer)

Death of a Staff Member

It is with great sadness that we come together today with the news of the death of _____. In this time of great sorrow and pain we turn to God and ask for strength. We pray for _____ that he/she may be granted eternal peace and happiness with an all-loving God. We pray for all family and friends that they be granted the strength to deal with this death. We pray for all of us, that we will find comfort and support in each other. May our faith offer us hope in this time of sorrow. With this in mind, we pray: (go to the opening prayer)

Opening Prayer

Lord God, source of all life, in this world and the next, we pray to you for our dear friend _____. Welcome him/her into the eternal joy of your kingdom. Give us all hope that one day we shall all be with you, our God, with _____, and with each other. There we will be united in your home, where there will be no tears, and our pain and sorrow will be turned into great joy. We ask this through Jesus our Lord and Savior. Amen.

Alternate opening prayer

Loving God, we ask that you hold _____ in the palm of your hands. May his/her soul find eternal rest and peace with you, our divine and almighty Savior. Grant his/her family the courage and strength that they need during this very difficult time. May the family be comforted through our support and through hope in the promise of eternal life which you have made possible through your own death and resurrection. We ask all this through you, Lord Jesus, our hope and our salvation. Amen.

Scripture Reading

We listen now to the story of Jesus' resurrection. This is a story that offers us great hope. It is a reminder of the great promise that Jesus has given to us, the promise of salvation, a promise of life everlasting, with an all loving, caring and compassionate God. A reading from the gospel according to Luke (24:1–8):

But on the first day of the week, at early dawn, the women came to the tomb, taking the spices that they had prepared. They found the stone rolled away from the tomb, but when they went in, they did not find the body. While they were perplexed about this, suddenly two men in dazzling clothes stood beside them. The women were terrified and bowed their faces to the ground, but the men said to them, "Why do you look for the living among the dead? He is not here, but has risen. Remember how he told you, while he was still in Galilee, that the Son of Man must be handed over to sinners, and be crucified, and on the third day rise again." Then they remembered his words.

Response   *Praise to you, Lord Jesus Christ.*

Concluding Prayer

Lord God, your gift of the body and blood of Christ
   is a sign of your unending love for your people.
May we be strengthened in our loss,
   may we be encouraged in the darkness of death,
   and live our lives in service to you.
We do all this in the hope that one day
   we will share in the risen life of Christ.
We make our prayer through Christ our Lord. Amen.

Alternate Prayer Service

This may be used when there is a close relationship between the students and the deceased.

Death of Either Student or Staff Member

"Blessed are they who mourn." This beatitude offers us comfort at this difficult time. We know that Jesus shares our suffering because he, too, suffered when he became one of us. In fact it is in and through his life, death, and resurrection that we find hope at this difficult time. We know that he loves us tenderly and walks with us every step of the way, ready to help and to heal us.

Opening Prayer

Dear God, the death of _____ is very difficult for us. We can no longer follow as _____ shares your eternal life. We know that your love is far greater and more powerful than ours. We pray that you give our friend _____ your peace and your joy. Let his/her memory be a light that shines within each of us as we continue on this earthly journey. We put our pain and sorrow before you, Lord, as we know that you are the source of comfort. We ask this through Jesus, your Son. Amen.

Reflection: Footprints in the Sand

I dreamed I was walking along the beach with the Lord, and across the sky flashed scenes from my life. For each scene I noticed two sets of footprints in the sand; one belonged to me, and the other to the Lord. When the last scene flashed before us, I looked back at the footprints in the sand. I saw that many times along the path of life, there was only one set of footprints. I also noticed that it happened at the lowest and saddest times in my life.

I questioned the Lord about it. "Lord, you said that once I followed, you would walk with me all the way, but I have noticed that during the most troublesome times in my life, there is only one set of footprints. I don't understand why, in the times when I needed you the most, you would leave." The Lord replied, "My precious child, I would never leave you during your times of trial and suffering. When you see only one set of footprints, it was then that I carried you."

Concluding Reflection

*At a time when we feel helpless we listen to the words of Henri Nouwen (*Out of Solitude*) and pray that each of us can be the friend he describes:*

When we ask ourselves which persons in our lives mean the most to us, we often find that it is those who, instead of giving much advice, solutions or cures, have chosen rather to share our pain and touch our words with a gentle and tender hand. The friend who can be silent with us in a moment of despair or confusion, who can stay with us in our hour of grief and bereavement, who can tolerate not knowing, not curing, not healing, and face with us the reality of our helplessness, that is a friend who cares.

.

Other Prayers in the Event of Death

Christ, look on those who have no hope because they do not know you; may they receive faith in the resurrection and in the life of the world to come.

Lord God, you are the glory of believers and the life of the just. Your Son redeemed us by dying and rising again. Let our departed brothers and sisters share the joys and blessings of the life to come. We ask this through our Lord Jesus Christ, your Son who lives and reigns with you and the Holy Spirit forever and ever. Amen.

Lord God, your gift of the body and blood of your Son Jesus is a sign of your unending love for us. May we be strengthened in the loss of all our loved ones, may we be encouraged in the darkness of death and live our lives in service to you as we hope to share in the risen life of Christ. Amen.

We pray for all those who appear to die senseless deaths. May they be held in God's loving embrace.

Dear God, we often witness injustices and tragedies that do not make sense to us. We pray today for all those who have lost their lives in such unexplained acts. May they be in God's wonderful embrace, and may those who mourn them be comforted in faith and in friendship. May each of us work toward bringing God's love and peace to this world. May our witness to God's love help bring others into closer relationship with you. Amen.

Prayers in the Event of Tragedy or Death

Beatitudes

Blessed are the poor in spirit,
  for theirs is the kingdom of heaven.
Blessed are those who mourn,
  for they will be comforted.
Blessed are the meek,
  for they shall inherit the earth.

Thematic Prayers for the School Year

Blessed are those who hunger and thirst for righteousness,
   for they will be filled.
Blessed are the merciful,
   for they will receive mercy.
Blessed are the pure in heart,
   for they will see God.
Blessed are the peacemakers,
   for they will be called children of God.
Blessed are those who are persecuted for righteousness' sake,
   for theirs is the kingdom of heaven.
Blessed are you when people revile you and persecute you,
   and utter all kinds of evil against you falsely on my account.
Rejoice and be glad,
   for your reward is great in heaven.

—Matthew 5:1–12

Prayer of St. Francis

Lord, make me an instrument of your peace.
Where there is hatred, let me sow love;
   where there is injury, pardon;
   where there is doubt, faith;
   where there is despair, hope;
   where there is darkness, light;
   and where there is sadness, joy.

O Divine Master,
Grant that I may not so much seek
   to be consoled as to console,
   to be understood as to understand,
   to be loved as to love.
For it is in giving that we receive,
   in pardoning that we are pardoned,
   and in dying that we are born to eternal life.

Serenity Prayer

God, grant me the serenity to accept the things I cannot change;
Courage to change the things I can; And wisdom to know the difference.

Today we turn to the gospel of Matthew: "Whatever you ask for in prayer with faith, you will receive" (21:22). Recognizing the power of prayer we pray: Have mercy on us, Lord; in your goodness grant us peace of mind and heart. Help us feel your presence at this difficult time and know that you are always there for us. Amen.

We come to you today, loving God, and thank you for the love and support you have shown us through the compassion of those around us. We know there are more difficult times ahead. However, we also know you are always there for us. It may be hard to recognize your presence and power, so we ask you to make your presence more evident in the lives of all those affected by this tragedy. May each of our acts of kindness and support be a means by which your love is made known. Amen.

Creation/Nature

Creator God, when we look around at some of the beauty that exists in nature, we know that something far greater than us is responsible. We see your infinite power and love in: beautiful mountains, thundering waterfalls, a simple flower. We also witness in nature the awesome wonder of everyday life. In the birth of a child, the love of a mother, father, and friend, the comforting and supporting spirit of a community. It is in these simple yet powerful miracles of creation that we turn to you, our God and Savior, with all of our fears, insecurities and doubts, knowing that with your love, we can overcome all. Amen.

We see your glory, Lord, in the wonderful nature that surrounds us. As the flowers begin to bloom and the sun shines, we think of Someone who is far greater than we are, Someone who is far more awesome. During this time of year nature reminds us of your presence and your love. May we constantly be aware of the great love that you offer us and respond to that love by respecting all that you have created. Amen.

Thematic Prayers for the School Year

Wonderful and awesome God, may we be touched by the beauty of your earth. May we long to work toward preserving this beauty. May its delicacy keep us in awe, the dependence of one creature on another move us to peace, and its tranquility keep us joyful. Amen.

Education

God of wisdom, help each of us in our desire to seek knowledge for the sake of service. May we see our education as a means to help others, to foster the social teaching of the Church, and to increase our ability to love. Help us work toward solidarity, dignity, and peace for each person and for each nation. Ultimately, may we see our education as a means of better understanding human beings, so that we can better serve each other in the love and spirit of Jesus our Savior. Amen.

As we read, listen, and observe, O Lord, help each of us integrate the gospel values with all that we learn. Give us the wisdom to recognize whatever runs contrary to the gospel message, the strength to take a stand against it, and the faith to lead others to choose the values that Jesus lived and taught. May those with special gifts in the area of technology and communication use these gifts to educate and catechize all nations. May the love that Jesus has for every person be made known, and modern methods of communication be used to help spread the mission and message of Jesus. Amen.

Psalms for Teens

I Trust You, Jesus

It is in you, Lord, that I place my trust.
Though I may walk in darkness
  and may experience great despair,
  I know that you are always there with me.
I may not always provide the best company
  but I know, Lord, that you love me without limit
  and are with me every step of the way.
For this Lord, I am grateful.

God Is My Joy

The Lord is my shepherd,
  he always leads me.
No matter what path I take,
  I know that the Lord is there to redirect me.
He does not cast judgment against me,
  he does not keep records.
There is simply love and a willingness to
  lead me and direct me.
This provides me with great comfort
  and confidence in who I am.
The Lord is full of forgiveness and love,
  how could I ever turn away?

Bless the Lord

Bless the Lord, for he shall comfort those who turn to him.
When I am lost, the Lord shall lead me,
  when I am in despair, the Lord shall comfort me,
  when I am in hatred, the Lord will extend his love,
  when I am in darkness the Lord will shed his light.
Who other than the Lord can offer this,
  love without limit, that holds no grudges?
His love always welcomes us.
How blessed is the Lord my God!

God's Guidance

Let us look to God who offers direction.
Think of how wonderful my actions
  if I look to God before I act.
Think of how wonderful my words
  if I look to God before I speak.
Think of how wonderful my accomplishments
  if I pray to God for strength and love.

Psalm of Thanks

Thank you, God, for the gift of love,
   thank you, God, for the gift of friendship,
   thank you, God, for the gift of food and shelter.
Thank you for the gift of nature,
   thank you, God, for the ability to have an education,
   thank you, God, for the gift of freedom.
For all these things I am truly grateful.

Rejoice

Rejoice in the Lord for he is good and his love endures forever.
We take time to rejoice in you, O Lord, giver of all gifts.
Your creation is beautiful to behold.
Creator of life and nature,
   source of love and goodness.
May we always recognize the blessings you provide and
   be a people who rejoice in you.

God Is Everywhere

God is in everything I see,
   in the beauty of a child's face,
   the small fingers a child possesses.
God is in the flower as it blooms,
   in the sun as it sets.
God is in the mountains that we see,
   in the oceans that surround us,
   in the moon that shines, and
   in the sky that covers us.
God is in each and every one of us,
   as our creator, our maker, our savior.

God's Presence

When we laugh,
  You, God, are there.
When we cry,
  You cry, too.
When we fall,
  You reach to lift us up.
When we struggle,
  You cheer us on.
When we are sad,
  You reach out to us.
Although we may not always see you, God,
  You are always there.

Jesus

Letter from Jesus to a Special Friend

I am writing to say how much I care for you and to say how much I want you to know me better. When you awoke this morning, I exploded a brilliant sunrise through your window, hoping to get your attention, but you rushed off without noticing.

Later, I noticed you were walking with some friends, so I bathed you in warm sunshine and perfumed the air with nature's sweet scent, and still you didn't notice me. As you passed by I shouted to you in a thunderstorm and painted a beautiful rainbow in the sky, and you didn't even look.

In the evening, I spilled moonlight onto your face and sent a cool breeze to rest you. As you slept I watched over you and shared your thoughts, but you were unaware that I was so near. I have chosen you and hope that you will talk to me soon. Until then, I remain near. I am your friend and love you very much.

I love you,

Jesus

Dear Jesus, you are our brother and our friend. You love us without limit and understand us completely. You became human while remaining God. It was your mission to bring God's kingdom and spread God's love. May we never be afraid to turn to you, knowing that you understand our weaknesses and accept us as we are. Thank you for the love, understanding, and forgiveness that you offer each of us. Amen.

Mary, Mother of God

Praise and glory to you, God, for you have given us your Son to save us from sin. We praise you for choosing Mary to be his mother. Her courage in believing your message and her faith in accepting your will inspire us. Help us to be like Mary; to follow your word and feel it in our hearts. May we love your Son and live out his message, overcoming all obstacles so we may live a faith-filled life. Amen.

Dear Mary, Mother of Jesus, thank you for your example. You loved your Son Jesus, more than life itself. You stood beside him in his pain, in his suffering, and in his death. This must have been extremely painful for you. However, your faith enabled you to endure all this and more. You are a woman of great faith, courage, and love. May we imitate the model that you have given to us. May we let go of our own desires and let God work within us. Amen.

Racism and Peace

God of peace, grant all your people a vision of peace. May our leaders be given the prudence to find peaceful resolution to conflict. May each of us use our gifts to promote peace. May all those who live in fear, feel comfort in the support that we offer in prayer. Amen.

God of love, today we pray that all violence in the world will end. We pray for a sense of calm in a time of great uncertainty. We pray that the world be given the gifts of peace and reconciliation. May love help us overcome all our fears so we can work together toward peace. Amen.

God of justice, may we listen to those around us who are different. Grant us the wisdom to learn from them and share their lessons. May we "open the doors of opportunity to all of God's children," no matter the color of their skin, the language they speak, the religion they practice, or the politics they live by. We ask this in the name of Jesus your Son. Amen.

Reconciliation and Forgiveness

God of forgiveness, as we prepare for the sacrament of reconciliation, help us better understand how we can live your love more faithfully and more fully. Give us the strength and courage to carry out your will. May we be thankful for all that we have been given and show it through a thoughtful reflection on how we can better serve you each day. Amen.

God of love, as we prepare for the sacrament of reconciliation, we ask your forgiveness for the times we have not responded to your love. Help us better imitate the love you have for each of us. May we be willing to forgive one another as you forgive us. Amen.

Vocations

Dear God, we know the love that you have for each of us. We pray today that we keep an open heart and mind and hear you when you are calling us. May we be willing to listen, and have the courage to respond. If we ourselves are not called to religious life, help us support and encourage those who are. We pray for them in a special way. Amen.

Dear Lord, we know that responding to your call is not easy; it takes great courage and great faith. Help each of us hear your call. May we be blessed with the support and direction in our own lives that help us say yes to you. Amen.

CHAPTER FOUR

Prayers for Feasts & Saints Days

September 3
Gregory the Great, pope and doctor (540?-604)

Patron of teachers, scholars, music, singers

Son of a wealthy Roman senator, St. Gregory was made prefect or governor of Rome in his early thirties. After five years he resigned and founded six Benedictine monasteries. At age fifty he was made Pope. He made peace with the invading Lombards, cared for the poor and the victims of the plague and famine, and made many reforms through his writings.

Dear God, give each of us the courage and strength we need to be true witnesses to our faith. Like Gregory the Great, help us understand the changes we can make through our courageous acts. May we always have the faith to be true witnesses to Jesus. Amen.

September 8
Birth of Mary, Mother of Jesus (first century)

Today we celebrate the birth of Mary. This feast originated in the Eastern Church. No one is certain where Mary was born. Some traditions say Nazareth and others Jerusalem. This feast celebrates Mary's personal sanctity and vocation as Mother of Jesus.

Dear God, the birth of the Virgin Mary's Son, Jesus, gave each of us the promise of salvation. Help us live the faith that Mary taught in accepting your will. May we have the strength to face all that discipleship requires and rejoice in the promise of salvation offered to each of us in and through Jesus' birth and life. Amen.

September 9
Peter Claver, priest (1581-1654)

Patron of missionary work among black people

This young Jesuit priest left Spain, his homeland, in 1610 to minister to the slaves in South America. Although condemned by the Church, the slave trade contin-ued. Peter Claver served the people both on and off the ship, bringing them medicines, food, bread, water, brandy, and lemons. He gave basic instructions of the faith and assured his brothers and sisters of their human dignity.

Dear Jesus, we know that like St. Peter, we are called upon to exercise courage. When we are challenged to stand up for what is right, help us accept this challenge. May our words be a voice for the weaker members of society. May our actions defend the rights of others. We know that we can find the courage to do this by developing a strong faith life. May you and your teachings always be at the center of all that we do and are. Amen.

September 13
John Chrysostom, bishop and doctor (349-407)

Patron of preachers, public speakers

Bishop of Constantinople. John suffered stomach ailments from his desert days as a monk. He returned to Antioch as a prophet and powerful speaker, speaking out against greed, injustice, and lack of concern for the poor. His sermons were so pow-erful that he comforted the disturbed and disturbed the comfortable.

God of holiness, we know that none of us is without fault. We each have our limitations and weaknesses, as well as gifts and strong points. Help us know our strengths and use them to serve you as St. John Chrysostom did. In doing your will may we be peacemakers who touch the lives of many. Amen.

September 14
Feast of the Triumph of the Cross

This feast day has been celebrated since the fourth century. On this day we honor the work of Christ. Because the three parts of the Paschal Mystery (suffering, death, and resurrection) are a single event in history, we look at the cross in light of the resurrection.

God of life, may we never be discouraged by the crosses that we face in our daily lives. Help us pick up our crosses as you did and walk confidently in faith and in love. May our struggles lead us to a deeper appreciation of life and help us be more understanding of the struggles of our friends. May we learn from the difficulties that we face and use this learning for the benefit of others. Amen.

September 15
Our Lady of Sorrows

This feast day was formerly known as the Seven Sorrows of Mary. The seven sorrows are: Simeon's prophecy at the presentation of Jesus in the temple, the flight into Egypt, the disappearance of the boy Jesus, the road to Calvary, the crucifixion, the removal from the cross, and the entombment of Jesus.

Dear God, often in life we face situations of sorrow and sadness; situations come that seem impossible to live with. Bless each of us with the strength to deal with all that life brings, as Mary did. Help each of us to see your love in every circumstance and the promise of salvation offered to each of us. We will never fully understand the reason for our suffering and turmoil. However, may we learn to cope with it, accept it, and carry on, in faith. Amen.

September 16
Cyprian, bishop and martyr (d. 258)

Patron of North Africa

Cyprian was the son of pagan parents, and became Christian at the age of twenty-five. He was a highly educated person, who became known as an orator. He was also known for his generosity in distributing his goods to the poor. Later,

Cyprian was chosen as Bishop of Carthage. During a plague there, he urged Christians to help everyone, including their enemies and persecutors. He was exiled by the emperor and then recalled for trial. He refused to leave the city, insisting that his people should have the witness of his martyrdom. Cyprian was a mixture of kindness and courage, vigor and steadiness.

Dear God, let us share in the gifts that you gave to St. Cyprian: kindness, courage, vigor, and steadiness. May our faith give us the confidence to use the gifts we have been blessed with. May we remain open to the Spirit in every action we take. Amen.

September 17
Robert Bellarmine, bishop and doctor (1542-1621)
Patron of catechists, catechumens

Robert was short in stature but a giant in academics. People would come from all over to hear him speak. While he occupied apartments in the Vatican, he limited his household expenses to what was barely essential, eating only the food available to the poor. For Pope Clement VIII he prepared two catechisms which had great influence in the Church.

Jesus, Lord and teacher, may we imitate the dedication to learning that St. Robert had. May we possess the fortitude to know when we should challenge contemporary values and to assert the values that you lived and spoke. May our faith give us the confidence to speak out when our voice needs to be heard. We ask this through Jesus our Lord and Savior. Amen.

September 21
Matthew, apostle and evangelist (first century)
Patron of bankers, accountants

Matthew was a Jew who worked for the Romans collecting taxes from his fellow Jews. Many tax collectors would keep much of the money they collected for themselves. Their fellow Jews viewed them as traitors. It was shocking to them when Jesus called Matthew to be one of his apostles. Matthew immediately left his job when Jesus called him.

God of forgiveness, help each of us recognize the times in our life when we have made mistakes. Give us the humility to see the error of our ways and the faith to turn our lives around. We know and trust in the forgiveness that you offer. May this forgiveness be a source of strength that encourages us to follow the path that we have chosen. Amen.

September 26 (celebrated October 19 in the US)
Jean de Brebeuf (1593-1649)

Patron of Canada

Today is the feast of St. Jean de Brebeuf and seven other martyrs of North America. They responded to a call to be missionaries to the Native Americans with great faith and courage. We pray today asking these martyrs to continue to pray for us. May we possess similar faith and courage.

Dear God, we are presented with many challenges in our lives. It is often difficult to know which direction to take, which challenges to accept and which to let go of. May we listen to the voice of the Spirit so we can be more confident in our decisions. May we not let fear cause us to turn away from these challenges. By accepting some of life's most difficult obstacles we receive some of its greatest rewards. Amen.

September 27
Vincent de Paul, priest (1580-1660)

Patron of works of charity, hospitals, prisoners

Vincent established homes of charity for the spiritual and physical relief of the poor and sick of each parish. He also founded homes for abandoned babies, several hospitals, collected relief funds for the victims of war, and ransomed over 1200 galley slaves from North Africa. He also conducted retreats for clergy at a time when there was great laxity. He was a pioneer in clerical training and instrumental in establishing seminaries.

Dear God, help all of us be compassionate people. When we look and see the needs that exist around us, let us not be overwhelmed. Instead, let us respond to that need by contributing in any way we can. May we have the strength and self-confidence to stand up for the oppressed and isolated, the teased and bullied, and bring them happiness and pride. May we rise to the challenges that surround us just as St. Vincent de Paul did. Then we will be filled with his joy and love. Amen.

September 29

Michael, Gabriel, and Raphael, archangels

Michael, Gabriel, and Raphael are three of the archangels who stand before God. The word angel means messenger, and archangel means a messenger sent by God on an assignment of great importance. The three angels mentioned in the Bible are: Michael, captain of the heavenly host, Gabriel, who announced to Mary that she would be the Mother of God, and Raphael, who guided Tobiah.

Dear God, may your angels be at our side to guide us as we make decisions throughout this day. Help us follow the direction they give us. May we feel the presence of your angels, and may this offer us comfort and support as we carry out your work here on earth. Amen.

September 30

Jerome, priest and doctor (345-420)

Patron of Scripture scholars, librarians, students

Jerome was known for his fiery spirit and bad temper, but his love for God and Jesus Christ was intense. He was a Scripture scholar, a master of many languages, translating the Old Testament from Hebrew and the New Testament from Greek. This translation of the Bible into Latin, the language of that day, was done by hand and took him over thirty years. He also wrote commentaries, which are a great source of inspiration for us today.

Dear God, we thank you for the many talents you have blessed us with. May we share the zeal of St. Jerome for your gospel, so that others may come to know about Jesus and about his love. God, give us the strength to keep doing the work of your saints and the perseverance to make your work our priority. Amen.

October 1
Thérèse of the Child Jesus, virgin (1873-1897)
Patron of foreign missions, France, florists, gardeners, aviators

Few saints of God are more popular than this young nun. She entered the convent of Lisieux, France, at age fifteen and died at the age of twenty-four. No matter what she did, scrubbing floors, sewing clothes, or cooking, she did it for God. Near the end of her life, Thérèse became ill with tuberculosis. Patient suffering became her mission. Thérèse said she came to the Carmel Convent "to save souls and pray for priests." Shortly before she died, she wrote: "I want to spend my heaven doing good on earth."

Dear God, as we progress in our daily routines, may we never lose sight of the gift of life. May we learn to appreciate each moment that we have, no matter how repetitive and busy our routines become. Help us see each moment as an opportunity to bring you to all those we encounter. The simplest of our gestures provide the greatest opportunities to make others aware of your love and presence in our lives. May we treasure each of these opportunities and demonstrate to others through our own acts what your face looks like. Amen.

October 2
Feast of the Guardian Angels

The word "angel" comes from the Greek word for messenger. Scriptures contain references to the activities of the angels. It is widely believed that people have an angelic being, a guardian angel, assigned to them.

Angel of God, my guardian dear,
   to whom God's love commits me here.
Ever this day, be at my side,
   to light and guard, to rule and guide. Amen.

October 4
Francis of Assisi, monk (1182-1226)
Patron of Italy, Italian merchants, ecologists

Born into a wealthy family, Francis gave up every material thing he had to the poor and felt the total freedom to say "Our Father in heaven." He founded the Franciscans to live as and to serve the poor, and to preach the gospel. His devotion and loyalty to the Church was absolute. Two years before his death at the age of forty-four, he received the stigmata of Christ in his hands, feet, and side.

Dear God, help each of us rid ourselves of selfish desires and seek only to please you. May we recognize that true peace and happiness are not found in wealth and possessions but in saying yes to your love. Give each of us the faith, courage, and strength to say yes to you. May we work toward building up your kingdom here on earth as St. Francis did. Amen.

October 7
Our Lady of the Rosary

The feast of Our Lady of the Rosary was introduced to commemorate the victory of the Christians over the Turks at the battle of Lepanto in 1571. This victory was attributed as an answer to prayer, since the Turkish navy was superior to the Christian forces. Now, however, the feast emphasizes the rosary as a Marian devotion which brings us closer to Jesus.

Dear Jesus, may we draw closer to your Mother Mary through the prayer of the rosary. In this prayer we meditate on the mysteries of your life and hers. Mary, we ask through your intercession a greater love for your Son. Keep us close to him and show us how to imitate him as you did. Amen.

October 9
John Leonardi, priest (1541-1609)

After his ordination John became very active in hospitals and prisons. He and his followers founded a new congregation of diocesan priests who worked to strengthen the faith of the people and do pastoral work. He published a summary of Catholic doctrine, established a seminary, reformed several religious orders, and started new ones. This priest became a great power for good in Italy.

L oving God, may we each use our gifts to serve you. May we show others your love and compassion, whether through writing, visiting the sick, or helping in a food kitchen. We know that whatever path we choose in life, we have opportunities to show others the love you have for each of us. Keep our minds and hearts open to these opportunities. May we use them as a means of making your gospel come alive. Amen.

October 15
Teresa of Avila, virgin and doctor (1515-1582)
Patron of Spain, those with headaches

Teresa joined the Carmelite Sisters when she was twenty years old. She received visions from God, calling her to reform this religious community. She began her own community of Sisters who lived as the poor did, wearing sandals, sleeping on straw mats, and eating no meat. Seventeen other convents were opened like this one. Teresa's relationship with God grew and she wrote many books on how to pray and love God better. She became the first woman declared a Doctor of the Church.

G od of life, may we recognize the talents you have graciously given us, and decide on the best way to use our talents to serve you. May St. Teresa be an inspiration to all of us. Perhaps you are calling us to become sisters or priests, deacons or brothers. Help us answer your call. Amen.

Prayers for Feasts & Saints Days

October 16
Margaret Mary Alacoque, virgin (1647-1690)

Margaret Mary was chosen by Christ to help the Church realize more about the love of God symbolized by the heart of Jesus. She entered the Order of Visitation nuns at the age of twenty-four and cared for the sick. She was criticized for being slow and clumsy but was also known to be humble, honest, patient, and kind. Jesus appeared to her many times and revealed that his human heart was to be the symbol of his divine and human love. By her own love she was to make up for the coldness and ingratitude of the world.

Heart of Jesus, no matter how difficult life becomes may we always know that you are there by our side. May we never place too much emphasis on the trials of this life. We know that this life is a short journey to you, and one day we will be united with you. May our knowledge of this promise of eternal life give us great joy and hope. Amen.

Alternate
October 16
Marguerite D'Youville

St. Marguerite knew what it was like to struggle. She was raised in a family that lived in poverty. However, she accomplished great things. She worked with three other Grey Nuns (as they became known) in sheltering needy women. She was put in charge of a hospital that was heavily in debt, and through her efforts the hospital was saved.

Dear God, no matter how difficult life becomes, we know you are always at our side. May we not place too much emphasis on the trials of life, but remember that this life is a short journey to you and that one day we will be united with you. May this promise of eternal life give us great joy and hope. We ask this through Jesus your Son. Amen.

October 17
Ignatius of Antioch, bishop and martyr (d. 107?)

Born in Syria, Ignatius converted to Christianity and eventually became bishop of Antioch. He is well known for his seven letters, five of which are to Churches in Asia Minor where he urges Christians to remain faithful to God and to obey their superiors. He warns them against heretical doctrines and provides them with the solid truths of the Christian faith. In his final letter he begs the Christians in Rome not to try to stop his martyrdom. "The only thing I ask of you is to allow me to offer the sacrifice of my blood to God." In the year 107 Ignatius bravely met the lions in the Coliseum.

God of hope, may our faith be strong. May St. Ignatius serve as a model and guide. When others challenge us, may we not compromise our values and beliefs. May we feel the true peace that faith offers and live this faith each day of our lives. Amen.

October 18
Luke, evangelist (first century)
Patron of artists, painters, doctors, sculptors

Luke wrote the third gospel and the Acts of the Apostles. In these two books he shows us the compassionate and forgiving Christ and the parallel between the life of Christ and that of the early Church. His gospel speaks of mercy, salvation, the poor, prayer, the Holy Sprit, and joy. He accompanied Paul on his dangerous journey to Rome.

Dear God, help us teach others about Jesus in all that we say and do. As St. Luke taught us through his actions, may we reach out to the poor and oppressed. Help each of us to be a voice for all those who have no voice. May our actions show the love, mercy, and forgiveness that you offer to all your people. Amen.

October 19
Paul of the Cross, priest (1695-1775)

Along with the compassion he naturally felt for the physical and spiritual pover-
ty of others, St. Paul also had a strong attraction toward contemplation, solitude,
and penance. He lived a life of discipline and would give up many things to share
in the passion and death of Jesus. After living for some time as a hermit, he
founded in Rome the Passionist Congregation, which is devoted to preaching
parish missions on the mystery of the cross. Paul received the gifts of prophecy and
healing. He taught us to carry our own cross with courage.

Dear God, may we take some time each day for private prayer with you.
May we be aware of your presence and may this encourage us to pray
regularly. We know that prayer takes many forms and that a few words spoken to you help us to get through each day. You accept us as we are. In our
busy lives help us understand how much you appreciate hearing from us.
Amen.

October 24
Anthony Claret, bishop (1807-1870)
Patron of weavers

Anthony was a missionary, religious founder, social reformer, queen's chaplain,
writer and publisher, archbishop and refugee. He became one of Spain's most pop-
ular preachers. At the age of forty-two, beginning with five young priests, he
founded a religious institute of missionaries, known today as the Claretians. He
was appointed to head the archdiocese of Santiago in Cuba. Fifteen assassination
attempts were made on his life for attempting to help black slaves and poor fam-
ilies better their lives.

Dear God, give us the same gifts of compassion and courage that you
gave to St. Anthony. May we each find the time to use these gifts as
St. Anthony Claret did, to build up your kingdom. Grant us direction, prudence, and confidence as we give of our time and our talents in loving service to you. Amen.

November 1
All Saints Day

November begins with a double feast in remembrance of those who have died. The saints, the people whom God has brought into heaven, are remembered on November 1, All Saints Day. Many of our own family members have died. They are also part of God's "harvest." We pray for all of them on November 2, All Souls Day. During these days we pray for all people who will one day share in the glory of all the saints.

God of all harvests and all happiness, we thank you for the festival of All Saints, for the saints who befriend us and teach us the way of the gospel. Keep our hearts open to those who need us. Help us gain strength and courage from the saints who have gone before us. Amen.

Alternate prayers for All Saints Day

Teach us and inspire us, Lord, to be people of charity, reaching out to those who are broken, feeding the hungry, clothing the naked, providing care for the homeless. Help each of us follow the example of the many saints who have gone before us. Amen.

On this feast day of All Saints, we pray that one day we, too, may share in the eternal glory of the saints. May their lives be an inspiration to each of us. Amen.

Dear God, help us look at the example of the saints who have gone before us. May we reflect on their faith and be inspired by their courage and determination. When we feel weak, help us gain the strength we need from the example of the saints, so we can respond to your call. Amen.

November 2
All Souls Day

Today is All Souls' Day, when we remember our relatives and friends who have died. Many of them are not famous, their statues are not in churches, but their pictures are in our homes and their stories are alive in our families. We know about their goodness and their struggles. They are alive in our hearts and in the way they have affected our lives. We pray for them and remember them with love.

God our creator and redeemer, by your power Christ conquered death and returned to you in glory. We pray today that all those we remember with love, who have gone before us in faith, may share in Christ's victory and enjoy the vision of your glory forever. Amen.

Alternate prayer for All Souls Day

Today is All Souls Day. Some of our family and friends have died, and we miss them very much. We take comfort knowing that we share in the power of Christ's resurrection. We pray that all our deceased family members and friends are in the loving embrace of our Lord and Savior.

Good and gracious God, we pray today for all the friends and family who have died. We pray that their souls rest in peace. For ourselves we ask that we find comfort in the family and friends we have here on earth. May our faith in the love you have for each of us be a source of strength on our journey. Amen.

November 3
Martin de Porres, religious (1579-1639)
Patron of social justice, education

Martin worked with the Dominicans as a "lay helper." After nine years, the example of his prayer and penance, charity and humility led the community to request that he be allowed to make full religious profession. Many of his nights were spent in prayer; his days were filled nursing the sick and caring for the poor. He treated all people equally, regardless of race, color, or status. He founded an orphanage and took care of slaves. His charity extended even to the animals.

Dear God, many of us find great joy in caring for others. Help each of us recognize the call to serve you as St. Martin de Porres did. Give us the wisdom to discern what direction our life should take and the courage to pursue what we believe is our calling. Amen.

November 4
Charles Borromeo, bishop (1538-1584)

Patron of catechists, catechumens, seminarians

Although part of a noble family, Charles chose to dedicate himself to the Church. Because of his intellectual qualities he was entrusted with several important offices in the Vatican. Later he was appointed Secretary of State with full charge of the administration of the papal states. St. Charles encouraged the Pope to continue the work of the Council of Trent when at several points it was on the verge of breaking up. Charles himself gave most of his money to charity, setting up orphanages, hospitals, homes for neglected women, seminaries, and colleges. When authorities fled during the plague, he stayed in the city to minister to the sick and dying.

Dear God, may we follow the example of St. Charles Borromeo and use our gifts to assist the Church. Help each of us recognize that we are Church. We each have something to contribute to make Church more meaningful and vibrant in our own lives and the lives of others. May we not become overwhelmed but offer our own ideas and gifts. It is through the help of each person that Church becomes an important and active part in the lives of all believers. Amen.

November 10
Leo the Great, Pope and doctor (400?-461)

He guided the Church against enemies both inside and outside. He corrected false teaching and spread the correct teaching about the two natures in the person of Jesus. With strong faith he also led the defense of Rome against barbarian attack, taking the role of peacemaker. Known for his spiritually profound sermons and writings, and his pastoral care of his people, many of his prayers and writings affected the Church's position of peace, justice, and truth.

Dear God, help each of us to be peacemakers. Grant us the gift of wisdom and the joy of peace. May our words and actions bring peace to others. Amen.

November 11
Martin of Tours, bishop (316?-397)

Patron of France, horses, horse-riders, beggars, wine growers

Though Martin wanted to be a priest, his father forced him to serve in the army at the age of fifteen. However, Martin lived more like a monk than a soldier. At the age of twenty-three he refused his war bounty and asked that he now be allowed to serve Christ. Eventually he was released from duty, was ordained, and served with great zeal in Milan. He then returned to France and established a monastery. The people pressured him to become bishop and he reluctantly accepted.

Dear God, give each of us the courage to do what we have to in order to fulfill your plan for us. May we be true to that voice that echoes in our hearts as St. Martin of Tours was. On this day, Remembrance Day, we take a moment to remember others who have given their time and even their lives for peace. May we also be willing to set aside our own selfish desires and follow the ways of love, peace, and joy as St. Martin did. Amen.

November 11

Veterans Day (Remembrance Day in Canada)

Loving God, today we honor the memory and lives of our sisters and brothers who have died in the wars of our nation. We thank the men and women who have served, and are serving in the military services of our country. We remember, too, all women and men who are peacemakers in our own lives and in the lives of others. We pray today for peace in our hearts and minds. Amen.

Dear God, you have called us to be people of peace. May we have the wisdom to make the choices that promote justice and lead to peace. May we keep an open heart and mind that enables the Holy Spirit to work in and through us. We ask that all those who have died fighting for peace may rest in your embrace, and that all those who mourn them may be comforted in your love. We ask all this through Jesus our Lord and Savior. Amen.

November 12
St. Josaphat, archbishop (1580?-1623)   .

*John Kuncewicz chose the name "Josaphat" upon entering the Order of St. Basil.
In 1609 he was ordained a priest, and in 1617 he was named as Archbishop of
Polotsk, Russia. He worked for the union of the Ukrainian Church with Rome.
Many opposed his efforts asserting that he was pushing Roman-style Catholicism on
the Ukrainian Church. He was killed in 1623 by his opponents, and in 1867
became the first Eastern saint to be formally canonized.*

Dear God, may we be able to accept and love others, no matter what
our differences are. May we give up our own way of doing things if
another way is better. Help us see each person as a child of God and learn
from everyone. May we try to be united in faith, in love, and in hope with
our friends, in imitation of St. Josaphat. May this help to build up your
kingdom here on earth. Amen.

November 13
Frances Xavier Cabrini, virgin (1850-1917)
Patron of immigrants, Italy

*Frances is the first United States citizen to be canonized. She founded the
Missionary Sisters of the Sacred Heart. The pope asked St. Frances to go to New
York City to work with the thousands of Italian immigrants. She faced many problems but gradually overcame them and over the next thirty-five years she founded
sixty-seven institutions on four continents. These were dedicated to caring for the
poor, the abandoned, the uneducated, and the sick. Seeing great need among the
Italian immigrants, she organized schools and adult education classes. She died of
malaria in her own Columbus Hospital in Chicago.*

Dear God, give us the eyes to see the beauty and goodness in every race,
in every culture, in every person. May our actions show that we accept
everyone as a child of God. Help us overcome our fears. May the support
and friendship we offer others make them feel welcome and bring out the
best in them. Amen.

November 15
Albert the Great, bishop and doctor (1206-1280)
Patron of scientists, philosophers, students

He is known as the master of Thomas Aquinas. Against his family's wishes he entered the Dominicans. Albert became known as a curious, honest, and brilliant scholar. He wrote books on natural science, logic, rhetoric, mathematics, astronomy, ethics, economics, politics, and metaphysics. He was so intelligent that his friends and colleagues called him "the Great." For Albert, life was filled with wonders to discover.

Dear God, we know that we each have different strengths and weaknesses. Help us accept the unique gifts you have given us. May we try to develop these gifts. Help us see how these gifts can serve your kingdom on earth. May we be willing to study hard, as St. Albert did, to know you and your creation better. Amen.

November 16
Margaret of Scotland, mother and queen (1045-1093)
Patron of Scotland

Margaret was married to King Malcolm of Scotland, and she helped him become a virtuous king. He left all domestic affairs to her and often consulted her in state matters. Margaret tried to improve the arts and education among the people. She looked to their physical needs as well. She believed that giving money to the poor was not enough—you also had to give your time. In her own spiritual life she had certain times for prayer, ate sparingly, and slept little in order to have time for devotions.

Loving God, give each of us the faith to accept our calling in life. If we, like St. Margaret, are called to help others by giving advice or by improving the home environment of our families, then give us the humility to accept this calling. Help us abandon our own selfish desires and try to do what you would do in every word and gesture. Amen.

November 17
Elizabeth of Hungary, religious (1207-1231)

Patron of Catholic charities, Franciscan Third Order, bakers

The daughter of the King of Hungary, Elizabeth chose a life of penance and asceticism. After her marriage she would take bread to hundreds of the poorest in the land. After her husband died she gave away much of the royal purse to the poor; because of this, her family members decided to throw her out of the palace. She later joined the Third Order of St. Francis, spending the remaining few years of her life caring for the poor in a hospital which she founded.

Dear God, give each of us compassion for the needy similar to that of St. Elizabeth of Hungary. May we see in the face of each hungry child and each struggling mother and father an invitation to reach out to them and offer our help. May our heart guide us as we say yes to those who are in need of our help. Amen.

November 21
Feast of the Presentation of Mary

This feast commemorates the presentation of the Blessed Virgin Mary in the Temple according to Jewish law. An apocryphal source tells us that Mary was three years old when her parents brought her to the Temple in Jerusalem to offer her to God, following the custom of the time. Her parents were inspired by a priest's vision and left her there to serve God.

Dear God, you are here among us. We can feel your presence if we open our minds and hearts. May we respond to your presence and your invitation to return your love. May we listen to our hearts as Mary's parents did and follow your voice inviting us into relationship with you. Amen.

November 22
Cecilia, virgin and martyr (second century)

Patron of music, musicians, poets

Cecilia is one of the most famous of the Roman martyrs. Her parents forced her to marry a Roman named Valerian. Through Cecilia's influence, Valerian and his brother were converted. All three were later put to death for their belief in Jesus. Cecilia sang in her heart and has become a symbol of the Church's conviction that good music is an important part of the liturgy.

Lord of song, may we have the courage to fight for what we believe in. May we have the wisdom to know what is important to us. May we have the strength to hold firm to our beliefs. Lord, give us the confidence to assert those beliefs before the world. May we, like St. Cecilia and many of the martyrs who have gone before us, put our faith before the things of the world. Amen.

November 23
Columban, abbot (543?-615)

Patron of Ireland

St. Columban is considered the greatest of the Irish missionaries. As a young man he faced strong temptations and sought the advice of religious people. After several years of seclusion and prayer, he traveled to Gaul with twelve missionaries. They won wide respect for their life of discipline, their preaching, and their commitment to charity and religious life. Columban established a number of monasteries in Europe which became centers of religion and culture. He founded the famous monastery of Bobbio in Ireland and wrote many well-known books.

Dear God, sometimes in life an event shocks us and causes us to look at our lives. This can result in a major conversion experience. Most of us, however, have smaller, less powerful experiences that move us and direct us in minor ways. We pray today that we always listen to the Spirit. May our lifelong conversion process move us towards a deeper and more committed relationship with you. May we avoid all those temptations that turn us away from you, and seek whatever brings us closer to you. Amen.

November 30
Andrew the Apostle (first century)

**Patron of Russia, Scotland, the Greek Church,
fisherman, fish dealers**

Andrew was St. Peter's brother. Andrew and Peter were both fishermen. Jesus called them both to be his apostles, fishers of men. They responded to Jesus' invitation. John the evangelist presents Andrew as a disciple of John the Baptist. Little is known about Andrew in the gospels. Legend has it that Andrew preached the Good News in what is now modern Greece and Turkey, and was crucified at Patras.

Dear Jesus, we know that you called people who others thought were least likely to be called. May we show similar dignity and respect to all people. May we not seek power and popularity. Instead, may we seek goodness, kindness, and love. Help us walk in the path of virtue. Amen.

December 3
Francis Xavier, priest (1506-1552)

Patron of missions, Australia, India, Pakistan

Ignatius of Loyola challenged the wealthy Francis to serve Jesus and find true hap-
piness. Together they vowed poverty, chastity, and apostolic service, in obedience
to the pope. Francis spent ten years in India, and later went to Japan, bringing
the faith to the people. Wherever he went, he lived with the poorest people, shar-
ing their food and rough accommodations. He spent countless hours serving the
sick and the poor, particularly the lepers. He had little time to sleep and even to
pray, but he was filled with God's presence and joy.

God of the poor, through St. Francis Xavier you have taught us that it is
through service to the poor, ministering to those who suffer, and healing the sick, that we find true joy. Help us, O God, be people of love. Amen.

December 6
Nicholas of Myra, bishop (d. 350?)

Patron of Greece, Sicily, Russia, bakers, brides, children, merchants, travelers, sailors

Both Eastern and Western churches honor St. Nicholas. The best known story
about him tells about his charity toward a poor man who was unable to provide
dowries for his three daughters. Rather than see them forced into poverty,
Nicholas secretly tossed three bags of gold through the poor man's window. Over
the centuries this particular legend evolved into the custom of gift-giving on the
saint's feast day. In English-speaking countries, St. Nicholas became, through
translation of other languages, our present-day Santa Claus.

Dear God, as Christmas approaches, the birthday of your Son Jesus, we
pray for a renewed heart. Give us a heart filled with love that goes to
any length to serve our brothers and sisters in Jesus. Amen.

December 7
Ambrose, bishop and doctor (340-397)

Patron of learning

St. Ambrose was born in Germany of a wealthy Roman family. He gave a share of his family's money to the poor and by his example and teaching, led the bishops to a simpler style of life. He dared Empress Justina to execute him when she tried to take his churches. In the midst of riots he both inspired and calmed his people with hymns. He scolded Emperor Theodosius and made him do public penance for his crimes. His sermons, writings, and personal life reveal him as an "other-worldly man involved in the great issues of his day."

Powerful God, when asked to make a difficult decision we pray for the courage to make the right one. When we have to take a position, may we have the courage to stand up for what we believe to be true. Amen.

December 12
Jane Frances de Chantal, wife, mother, and religious founder (1562-1641)

Jane married at the age of twenty-one and had six children, three of whom died in infancy. At her castle residence she restored the custom of daily Mass and carried out various charitable works. After her husband's death, she met Francis de Sales, who became her spiritual director. She joined his community for women, carrying out works of mercy. She served the victims of the plague with all the resources of her convent. At times she felt far from God, but she kept her faith in him.

Loving God, sometimes we face hardships that make us want to give up. Give us the will power and stamina of Jane Frances. May we always be people of love, holding on through the most difficult times because we know the joy that awaits us in you. Amen.

December 13
Lucy, martyr (304)

Patron of those with eye trouble, writers, Sicily

Growing up in a pagan world in Sicily was difficult for Lucy. Her friends mocked her because of her faith. However, she held strong to her beliefs. She was martyred in 304.

Dear God, we pray to have the same kind of courage St. Lucy showed. When our friends mock us, when society criticizes us, we pray that we always remain strong in our love of and faith in you and the truths you taught us. Amen.

December 14
John of the Cross, priest and doctor (1542-1591)

Patron of diocesan priests

John was a reformer, mystic-poet, and theologian-priest. He worked for reform in his religious order. Because of that, he suffered opposition, misunderstanding, persecution, and imprisonment. He came to know the meaning of the cross—to experience the dying of Jesus—as he sat month after month in his dark, damp, narrow cell with only his God. He never grew bitter or resentful. The path to union with God means that the cross leads to the resurrection. If you want to save your life, you must lose it for Jesus' sake.

Lord of love, many small challenges are given to us daily and many difficulties are put in our way. We know that if our faith is strong, we can face all of these with peace, for you are with us always. Amen.

December 26
Stephen, first martyr (d. 36)

Patron of deacons, bricklayers, stone masons

The apostles asked the community to choose seven prudent and deeply spiritual men. Among those chosen was Stephen, a man filled with faith and the Holy Spirit. Stephen worked great wonders among the people. He was brought before the Sanhedrin. His speech made the crowd angry and they stoned him to death. As he was being killed, he prayed, "Lord Jesus, receive my spirit…Lord, do not hold this sin against them."

Dear God, fill every moment of my day with the Holy Spirit. May your Spirit bring the gifts of wisdom, prudence, tolerance, patience, and love. Amen.

December 27
John, apostle and evangelist (first century)

Patron of Turkey, protection against poisons

John was privileged to be present at the Transfiguration, the raising of the daughter of Jairus, and the agony in Gethsemane. He is best known for his great gospel, his letters, and the Book of Revelation. His gospel has great depth and is a very personal account. He sees the glorious and divine Jesus already in the events of his mortal life. At the Last Supper, Jesus speaks in John's gospel as if he were already in heaven.

Dear Jesus, John was your beloved disciple. He became known for his saying, "Little children, love one another, and you will fulfill the law of Christ." May we follow his example of love for you and for all our sisters and brothers. Amen.

December 29
Thomas à Becket, bishop and martyr (1118-1170)

Thomas was made archdeacon of Canterbury, then named chancellor of England at the age of thirty-six by his friend King Henry II. Thomas later became archbishop of Canterbury but he resisted the king's intrusion into Church affairs and Church rights. Thomas rejected the king's Constitution, which gave the king power over the Church, and he had to flee to France for safety. He returned seven years later and refused to withdraw the excommunication he had placed upon bishops favored by the king. Four of the king's knights killed Thomas in the Canterbury cathedral.

Dear Lord, grant us the faith to be true to you. When people in positions of power pressure us to compromise our beliefs, grant us the courage and prudence to follow your way. Amen.

December 31
Sylvester I, pope (d. 335)

Sylvester's papacy lasted from 314-335. In 313, under Emperor Constantine, the Edict of Milan put an end to the persecution of Christians. Pope Sylvester was a very strong and wise man. He basically kept the Church's affairs free from interference from the Emperor. During this period we see the Church coming out of the catacombs. We see the building of great basilicas, the Council of Nicea, and other critical events. Sylvester teaches us valuable lessons on good leadership.

Dear God, there are many who speak badly of the Church and its members. Give me the spirit of tolerance, a heart of forgiveness, and the courage to defend you and all that I believe to be true. Amen.

January 1
Mary, Mother of God

World Day of Prayer for Peace

In the gospels we learn that the angel Gabriel came to Mary and announced she would be the mother of Jesus. When Mary went to visit Elizabeth, Elizabeth greeted her as "the mother of my Lord." Mary asked Jesus to work his first miracle at the wedding at Cana. She was also at Jesus' crucifixion. Mary is the first and greatest among all saints.

Hail, Mary, full of grace, the Lord is with you. Blessed are you among women, and blessed is the fruit of your womb, Jesus. Holy Mary, mother of God, pray for us sinners, now and at the hour of our death. Amen.

January 2
Basil the Great, bishop and doctor (329-379)

Patron of hospital administrators

Basil founded the first monastery in Asia Minor, and his teachings influence Eastern monasticism today. He fought the error called Arianism, which denied the divinity of Christ. Basil was tireless in pastoral care. He preached twice a day to huge crowds, built a spectacular hospital, organized famine relief, worked in the soup kitchen, and fought the white slave market. Basil is considered a great preacher and teacher of the Church.

Lord God, I am afraid to get up and speak in front of people. Give me strength and courage to speak with wisdom so that everything I say reflects your goodness and love. May speaking your truth give me confidence and strength. Amen.

January 4
Elizabeth Ann Seton, wife, mother, religious founder (1774-1821)

Elizabeth Seton is the first person born in the United States to be declared a saint. When her husband died, Elizabeth was widowed and penniless with five small children to support. In 1805 she converted to Catholicism and opened a school in Boston. She founded the first American religious community for women, opened the first American parish school, and established the first American Catholic

... ...d two great devotions: abandonment to the will of God and an ... ...ssed Sacrament.

... ... I pray that I will never leave you even in the hardest times. ... ... you would never abandon me. You are always with me and ... ...ng me. We are next to each other, like parent and child, and we ... ...gether forever; loving each other to the end of time. Amen.

January ...

John Neumann, bishop (1811-1860)

John grew up and studied in Bohemia. He came to New York at the age of twenty-five and was ordained a priest. He did missionary work throughout the U.S. He first worked in Buffalo, New York and then in Philadelphia. He played a key role in the growth of Catholic schools which in eight years grew from two schools to one hundred. He was well known for his holiness and learning, his spiritual writing and preaching. He has been most admired for his great humility.

Dear God, you have given me the gift of a special talent. You have created me to do something special for you. May I listen to you faithfully and with love. Amen.

January 12

Feast of the Baptism of Our Lord

We reflect today on Jesus being baptized by John in the river Jordan, remembering God's words: "This is my Beloved Son, with whom I am well pleased" (Matthew 3:17).

January 17

Anthony of Egypt, abbot (251-356)

Patron of butchers, skin diseases

Anthony sold his inheritance and gave it all to the poor. He gave the Church and the world the witness of a life of solitude, personal self-sacrifice, and prayer. At the same time many people were drawn to him for spiritual healing and guidance. Anthony established a monastery and fearlessly exposed himself to danger while he helped those in prison during the Roman persecution.

Dear Jesus, there is terrible poverty in the world. Yet, you created a world rich enough to feed everyone. May I always be generous of heart and feed those who are hungry. May I always be willing to share what I have to help others live. Amen.

January 20
Sebastian, martyr (257?-288?)

Patron of athletes, soldiers, police, physicians

Sebastian was a Roman martyr. Legend says that Sebastian entered the Roman army only because in that position he could assist the martyrs without arousing suspicion. He was found out and delivered to archers to be shot to death. Sebastian recovered but refused to flee. He later confronted the emperor, denouncing him for his cruelty to Christians. This time the sentence of death was carried out. Sebastian was beaten to death with clubs.

Dear God, what great perseverance Sebastian had. My prayer today is that when times are tough and nothing seems to be going my way, I will never give up. Help me endure the difficult times and stand up for what I believe to be right. Amen.

January 21
Agnes, virgin and martyr (d. 304)

Patron of young girls, children of Mary

Agnes was martyred at age thirteen in the third century. A man wanted to marry her, but she would not. He reported her as a Christian. She was arrested and forced to go to a house of prostitution. When that failed, Agnes was then executed in Rome. Before her death she forgave the man who betrayed her. The daughter of Constantine built a basilica in her name.

Dear God, give us the kindness to forgive others who wrong us. May we be humble and faithful in our service to you. May we try to act justly, love tenderly, and walk humbly with you always. Amen.

January 24
Francis de Sales, bishop and doctor (1567-1622)

Patron of journalists, editors, writers, the deaf

Francis studied to be a lawyer, but instead decided to become a priest. He set out to convert Calvinists by preaching and writing and distributing pamphlets explaining the true Catholic doctrine. As bishop he continued to preach, hear confessions, and catechize children. His struggle to control his anger and be gentle was a great asset in winning souls. He wrote popular books, articles, and pamphlets and because of this he has been named patron of the Catholic press.

Dear God, it is gentleness that will have a great effect on stress. Teach me to be gentle. I pray for gentleness in my words and in my actions. I pray that my gentleness will bring comfort and healing to others. Amen.

January 25
Feast of the Conversion of Paul, the Apostle

For years he arrested, persecuted, imprisoned, and executed Christians. Knocked off his horse by a blinding light, Paul faced Jesus and was converted. From this point on Paul dedicated his life to Christ and established churches throughout the known world. Paul's message is that you are saved entirely by God, not by anything you can do.

Dear Jesus, you come to all of us in different ways. You offer us, like Paul, an opportunity to convert. I pray that my heart is always open to you and each experience with you is a conversion, making me a better person. Amen.

January 26
Titus, bishop (d. 94?)

Titus is seen as a peacemaker, administrator, and a great friend and disciple of St. Paul. We discover from Paul's letters what a source of strength he was for Paul. He helped Paul through difficult times and showed a unique ability to smooth out challenging situations.

Dear Lord, we see a lot of violence and war in the world we live in. We pray to be peacemakers, to bring people together in a spirit of tolerance and understanding. We pray for a world of harmony and unity. Amen.

January 28
Thomas Aquinas, priest and doctor (1225-1274)

Patron of Catholic schools, students, colleges, philosophers, and theologians

Thomas Aquinas is one of the greatest teachers of the medieval Catholic Church, and his writings are among the Church's treasures. The unity, harmony, and continuity of faith and reason, of revealed and natural human knowledge, pervades his writings. The Summa Theologica, *his last and, unfortunately, incomplete work, deals with the whole of Catholic theology.*

O God of knowledge, Thomas Aquinas was born with a brilliant mind. He used his gift to create a better world through his writings. I pray that I will use my intelligence to write and speak in a way that gives people hope and builds up your kingdom on earth. Amen.

January 31
John Bosco, priest (1815-1888)

Patron of editors, young people

Educator John Bosco advocated frequent celebration of the sacraments of penance and the Eucharist. He combined catechetical training and fatherly guidance, seeking to unite spiritual life with one's work, study, and play. After serving as a chaplain in a hospice for working girls, John opened the Oratory of St. Francis de Sales, for boys. He taught them various trades, including the publication of religious and catechetical pamphlets. He founded the Salesians, whose efforts concentrated on education and missionary work. Later he began a group of Salesian Sisters to assist girls.

L ord, you call me to serve. Keep my ears and heart open to your calling. You may be inviting me to be a priest or sister or brother, married or single. I am open to your call, Lord, and desire to serve you. Amen.

February 2
Feast of the Presentation of Our Lord

This feast celebrates the coming of the Lord into his temple. He is met by representatives of the old covenant: Simeon and Anna.

Lord of ages, my eyes have seen your salvation which you have prepared in the presence of all peoples, a light for revelation to the Gentiles and for glory to your people, Israel" (Luke 2:30–32).

February 3
Blaise, bishop and martyr (d. 316)

Blaise was a good bishop, working hard to encourage the physical and spiritual needs of the people. However, because persecution of Christians still raged in Armenia, Blaise was forced to flee to the back country. He lived there as a hermit in solitude and prayer. One day hunters found him and hauled him off to prison where a mother came with her young son who had a fish bone lodged in his throat. At Blaise's command the child was able to cough up the bone. The legend continues that the governor tried to persuade Blaise to sacrifice to pagan idols. Finally he was beheaded.

On this feast day we have the opportunity to have our throats blessed in church.

Dear Jesus, I pray that my life and the lives of my family and friends will be blessed with good health, peace, and love. When confronted with illness or obstacles, may we accept and overcome them through your comfort and love. Amen.

February 5
Agatha, virgin and martyr (d. 251)

Patron of Sicily, nurses, foundry workers, miners, jewellers

Legend has it that Agatha was arrested as a Christian, tortured, and sent to a house of prostitution to be mistreated. She was preserved from being violated, and was later put to death. The year after her death, the stilling of an eruption of Mount Etna was attributed to her intercession. As a result, apparently, people continued to ask her prayers for protection against fire.

Loving Lord, protect me and my family from evil and all those elements that bring destruction. Keep us safe in your loving arms. Amen.

February 6
Paul Miki, priest and martyr, and Companions, martyrs (1564-1597)

Paul Miki was a Jesuit and native of Japan. He was martyred along with many others in Japan. He was martyred because he taught the doctrine of Christ. He preached to people that they should not hesitate to ask Jesus to help them to be happy. He forgave those who persecuted and killed him.

Dear God, many will challenge us for being who we are and having the beliefs we have. May we stand strong in our faith and connections, holding fast to what we believe to be true and right. Amen.

February 8
Jerome Emiliani, religious (1481-1537)

Patron of orphans, abandoned children

While spending time in prison, Jerome learned to pray. When he escaped, he returned to Venice and began to study for the priesthood. Plague and famine swept northern Italy. Jerome distributed all his property and possessions to the needy, particularly to abandoned children. He founded three orphanages, a shelter for penitent prostitutes, and a hospital. He later founded a congregation dedicated to the care of orphans and the education of youth.

Dear Lord, I pray every day that my spirit and my soul will be nourished. I pray that I will always be meditative and reflective, with an open heart and clear mind. Amen.

February 10
Scholastica, virgin, religious (480-542?)

Patron of children with convulsions

Scholastica and her twin brother St. Benedict both established religious communities close to each other. She was born of wealthy parents but gave up her wealth to live as a poor contemplative. Scholastica and her brother kept in close contact throughout the year. They were a great spiritual support for each other.

L oving Lord, may my love and union with my siblings always be strong, so I can be for them a constant support and a source of love and inspiration. Amen.

February 11
World Day of Prayer for the Sick

Jesus wanted the people to know that God wants our total good as human beings. Jesus forgave people their sins and ministered to the sick. The Church has designated today as World Day of Prayer for the Sick. We pray for healing. It is also a day to recognize the selfless work of doctors, nurses, and other health-care specialists who dedicate their lives to healing others.

D ear Jesus, you healed the blind, the lame, the crippled, people afflicted with different kinds of pain and illness. We pray to you for healing of our physical as well as our spiritual afflictions. Help us bring comfort, support, and love to all those who are ill. Amen.

February 21
Peter Damian, bishop and doctor (1007-1072)

Damian lived a life of prayer and fasting. He eventually left teaching and gave himself to prayer with the Benedictines. He prayed often, studied the Bible, and slept rarely. As abbot he found five other hermitages. He often served as a peacemaker between arguing factions in the Church or government. He was eventually made cardinal-bishop of Ostia and wrote many letters, sermons, and biographies.

L ord of all, you call us to be a brother or sister to all people. You give us a moral obligation to love all of your children. We pray for the courage to bring about justice and peace. Amen.

February 22
Feast of the Chair of Peter

This feast commemorates Christ's choosing Peter to take his place as the servant-authority of the whole Church. Peter is the spokesman for the Twelve about their experience of the Holy Spirit; before the civil authorities to defend the Church's mission; for the community in the problem of Ananias and Sapphira. Peter is the first to preach the good news to the Gentiles. The healing power of Jesus in him is well attested in many miracles. On Vatican Hill, in Rome, during the reign of Nero, Peter died as a martyr, probably in the company of many Christians.

D ear God, we pray for healing powers, that is, words and actions that bring healing to others, to their physical, mental, and spiritual afflictions. Amen.

February 23
Polycarp, bishop and martyr (60?-156)

Polycarp was a disciple of St. John the Apostle and friend of St. Ignatius of Antioch. He was a revered Christian leader during the first half of the second century when he became bishop of Smyrna. The Asia Minor churches recognized Polycarp's leadership by choosing him as a representative to discuss the date of the Easter celebration in Rome. He wrote many letters in the early Church but only his letter to the Philippians has been preserved. At the age of eighty-six, Polycarp was led into the crowded Smyrna stadium to be burned alive and finally killed by a dagger.

G od of hope, my greatest desire is to do good. If all that I do and say is good, I will, in some way, contribute to a better world. Amen.

March 4
Casimir (1458-1483)

Patron of Poland, Lithuania, Russia

Born of kings and in line to be a king, Casimir was blessed with many virtues, including knowledge. Even as a teenager he was known for his goodness, and lived a disciplined life, sleeping on the ground, spending a great part of the night in prayer, and dedicating himself to lifelong celibacy. At one time he was sent by his father to lead an army into war but he refused. He returned home and made the decision never to involve himself in war.

Dear God, it is difficult to live a life of self-control. I know that this is what you call me to, and this discipline will bring many rewards. However, I sometimes give in to temptation. When I fail, I pray for a reconciled and renewed relationship with you. Amen.

March 7
Perpetua and Felicity, martyrs (d. 203)

Perpetua was a young, beautiful, well-educated mother, and chronicler of the persecution of the Christians by the emperor Septimius Severus. Felicity was a courageous slave in the prison and was pregnant. Despite threats of persecution and death they both refused to renounce the Christian faith. They were sent to the public games in the amphitheater where they were set upon by bears, then beheaded. In her diary, Perpetua describes her period of captivity as a time of horror. However, when they allowed her infant son to stay with her, her prison became a palace to her.

Dear Lord, there are times when I feel like everything is going wrong and there is nobody who believes in me or supports me. I know you are always with me and my friendship with you comforts me. Thank you for your unconditional love and constant presence. Amen.

March 8
John of God, religious (1495-1550)

Patron of hospitals, the sick, nurses, booksellers, those with heart ailments

John led a wild life until he was forty. His acts of penance were as passionate as his previous life had been. Then he was visited by Blessed John of Avila who advised him to be more actively involved in tending to the needs of others rather than in enduring personal hardships. John gained peace of heart and began his work with the poor. He established a house for the sick and the poor and continued a deep interior prayer life reflected in his spirit of humility. Twenty years after his death his followers formed the Brothers Hospitallers.

Loving Lord, I will do acts of charity and goodness to reconcile my relationship with you and those who I have offended. I will sacrifice my own selfish desires to show you how much I desire to live in union with you. Amen.

March 9
Frances of Rome, wife, mother, and religious (1384-1440)

Patron of widows, motorists

A devoted and loving wife, Frances longed for a life of prayer and service, so she organized a group of women to minister to the needs of Rome's poor. With the birth of her children she turned her attention to the needs of her own household. When the great plague struck Italy, Frances used all her money and sold all her possessions to buy whatever the sick might need. She was then given permission to found a society of women who offered themselves to God through service to the poor. She joined the community after her husband died.

Dear God, you call some of us to be leaders. If I am chosen to be a leader, may I lead with wisdom and prudence. Amen.

March 17
Patrick, bishop (389?-461?)

Patron of Ireland, Nigeria

At the age of sixteen Patrick and a large number of his father's slaves and vassals were captured by Irish raiders and sold as slaves in Ireland. For six years he worked as a shepherd, suffering from hunger and cold, until he escaped. His captivity had meant spiritual conversion and after years of study he was made bishop. He felt the call to work in Ireland, and returned there and converted many to Catholicism. He ordained a large number of priests, divided the country into dioceses, held church councils, founded several monasteries, and continually urged his people to greater holiness in Christ. He was a man of action, with a rock-like belief in his vocation.

Lord of the missions, you call us to be a servant to all your people. As St. Patrick brought you to the Irish, may we, through our acts of faith and love, bring all people to you. May we embrace our suffering, enduring it as you endured the cross. May our suffering forge greatness within and bring us the treasures of the heart. Amen.

March 18
Cyril of Jerusalem, bishop and doctor (315?-386)

Ordained a priest and given the task of catechizing those preparing for baptism, Cyril was later accused of insubordination and of selling Church property to relieve the poor. After being vindicated, he returned to find Jerusalem torn with heresy, schism, and strife, and racked with crime. He went to the (second ecumenical) Council of Constantinople, where the amended form of the Nicene Creed was promulgated. As a result of his work there, the bishops of the Council praised him as a champion of orthodoxy against the Arians who were denying the divinity of Jesus.

Dear God, there are times when people tell false stories and lies about me or other people. Help me to stand up for the truth. I know you are with me, and I pray that all I do is true to you. Amen.

March 19
Joseph, husband of Mary (first century)

Patron of the Church, fathers, carpenters, artisans, manual workers, the poor, priests, religious, travelers

The Bible pays Joseph the highest compliment, saying Joseph was a "just"man. By this the Bible means that he was completely open to all that God wanted. He became holy by surrendering totally to God. This just man was simply, joyfully, wholeheartedly obedient to God—in marrying Mary, in naming Jesus, in shepherding the precious pair to Egypt, in bringing them to Nazareth, in the undetermined number of years he lived and worked with faith and courage.

Jesus, give me the strength, courage, and wisdom to be a just person like St. Joseph. May my actions, words, career, and all my life choices express justice toward others and bring about justice in my community. Amen.

March 23
Turibius of Mongrovejo, bishop (1538-1606)

Patron of Latin American bishops

Turibius was ordained priest and bishop and sent to Peru where he found colonialism at its worst. The Spanish conquerors, including some of the clergy, were guilty of every sort of abuse against the native population. Turibius visited everywhere, studying the language and staying two or three days in each place with neither bed nor food, facing wild animals, disease, and hunger. Many of his people were very poor, yet sensitive, so he helped them secretly, while speaking out against abuses and building hospitals.

Dear Jesus, you call us to be a people of charity, giving to the poor quietly, without boasting of our charitable acts. Help me be a person who acts quietly and humbly, serving others because of my love for you. Amen.

April 2
Francis of Paola, hermit (1416-1507)

Patron of seafarers

Francis loved solitude and lived as a contemplative hermit in a remote cave over-looking the sea. He established a community and called this community the "Minims" meaning: "least in the household of God." Humility, as well as self-denial, was to be their hallmark, along with the religious vows of poverty, chastity, and obedience. Later, when he felt called to apostolic life, he began to use his gifts of miracles and prophecy to minister to the people, especially the poor and oppressed.

Loving God, may we remain humble in all we do. May we learn to follow your way, not ours. We ask this though Jesus, our Lord and Savior. Amen.

April 7
John Baptiste de la Salle, priest (1651-1719)

Patron of teachers

Though he could have had an easy life and a high position in the Church, God had other plans for John. John began to see his mission as the establishment of schools for poor boys. He left home and family, gave away his fortune, and devoted himself completely to working with the poor. He founded the "Brothers of the Christian School," a community that educated boys of poor families and set up homes and schools for delinquent children. John dedicated his life completely to what he believed was God's calling for him.

Dear God, bless all of our teachers. May they be given the strength and faith to teach us in both words and actions. May our efforts to learn encourage them in their mission. Amen.

April 21
Anselm, bishop and doctor (1033-1109)

Anselm lived a worldly life for years until, at the age of twenty-seven, he finally entered the monastery. He was chosen abbot and became one of the Church's greatest theologians and leaders. He was an original and independent thinker,

Prayers for Feasts & Saints Days

admired for his patience, gentleness, and teaching skill. His abbey became a monastic school, influential in philosophy and theology. He published many of his own works. He was later appointed Archbishop of Canterbury and met with much opposition from the king of England because the king would not work with Anselm for Church reform.

L oving God, each day may our hearts be open to your call. We do not know what our future holds, and live each day in wonder and excitement. May we have the courage and strength to say yes to you. Amen.

April 24
Fidelis of Sigmaringen, priest and martyr (1577-1622)

Patron of lawyers

Fidelis was a lawyer who fought for the rights of the poor and the oppressed. Eventually he became so disgusted with the corruption and injustice he saw among his colleagues that he dropped his law career and became a Franciscan priest. His own wealth was divided amongst needy seminarians and the poor. He devoted the rest of his life to caring for the sick and the poor. He was eventually killed by a group who opposed his work and philosophy. Fidelis' prayer in life was that he always remain faithful to God and not give in to apathy.

D ear God, give us the strength to remain true to our convictions and beliefs. When we are put in a position of compromise, may we exercise prudence and never be unfaithful to ourselves or to you. We know that true peace and happiness are attained in and though your ways. Amen.

April 25
Mark, evangelist (first century)

Mark is the author of the oldest and shortest of the four gospels. His gospel was written for Gentile converts in Rome between 60 and 70 AD. The apostle Peter is believed to be one of his sources as well as the Church in Jerusalem and Antioch. Mark was not one of the twelve apostles. We are not sure if he knew Jesus personally. Mark and Paul knew each other well as he accompanied Paul on Paul's first missionary journey. Later Paul requested that Mark visit him in prison. One of Mark's gospel themes is his emphasis on Jesus' rejection by men while being God's triumphant envoy. He also speaks of Jesus as the suffering Son of God, willing to suffer death for our salvation.

Dear God, may we always be willing to use our gifts in your service. Help each of us make your word come alive here on earth and in all that we say and do. Amen.

April 28
Peter Chanel, priest and martyr (1803-1841)
Patron of Oceania

Peter wanted to be a missionary and joined the Society of Mary. After teaching for years in a seminary he was sent to work on Futuna Island. He spent five years there working with whalers, traders, and warring natives. Despite what appeared to be little success he kept a serene and gentle spirit, endless patience, and courage. Some of the natives began fighting with others and Peter Chanel became one of the victims. Within two years after his death the whole island became Catholic.

Dear God, help us persevere when we are discouraged. May we never be overcome by any of life's challenges. When our contributions feel minimal, help us to feel your presence. May we remain humble and faithful in all we do. Amen.

April 29
Catherine of Siena, virgin (1347-1380)
Patron of Italy, fire prevention

Against her mother's wishes, Catherine chose not to marry and spent hours in her room praying and fasting. At sixteen she joined the Third Order of St. Dominic and spent the first three years in seclusion and prayer. This changed when Jesus spoke to her and told her to serve others. She then visited prisoners, fed the poor, nursed patients no one would touch, and buried the dead. Although she could not read or write she dictated two books and more than 400 letters. She became widely recognized for her gifts of prophecy, spiritual guidance, writings, and peacemaking abilities.

God of love, give us the courage to take a stand when our voice is needed. Let us not be intimidated or frightened by people or organizations that get in the way of carrying out your will. Help us recognize the power of prayer and make prayer a regular part of our day. Amen.

April 30
Pius V, pope (1504-1572)

Pius V had the overwhelming responsibility of getting a shattered and scattered Church back on its feet. The Church had been shaken by the Reformation and corruption. Pius V had the challenge of now implementing the sweeping reforms called for by the Council of Trent. He founded seminaries for the proper training of priests; published a new missal, a new breviary, a new catechism; enforced legislation against abuses in the Church; built hospitals for the sick and the poor; provided food for the hungry; and rerouted Church money to poor convents. Reforming Church and State was no easy task. He spent long hours in prayer, fasted rigorously, deprived himself of many papal luxuries, and observed the Dominican Rule.

Loving God, when we witness injustices or abuses in life, give us the courage and wisdom to take a stand against these actions. May justice and fairness serve as our mandate. When your word becomes obscured or misinterpreted, may we remain open to the spirit. We ask this through our Lord and Savior. Amen.

May 1
Joseph, the Worker

Jesus was a carpenter and was trained by his father Joseph. This profession had many satisfactions as well as many drudgeries. Joseph and Jesus are carpenters and their work involves being creative. We are called to use our hands and minds to serve God. Ultimately our creations are for the purpose of building God's kingdom. An exemplary father, Joseph worked hard for his family, found meaning and vocation in his work and lived in close communion with his family.

Dear God, may our gifts and talents be used to build up your kingdom here on earth. May all we make reflect your love, your goodness and your beauty. Amen.

May 3
Philip, apostle (first century)

Patron of Uruguay

Like many of the other apostles, Philip took a long time to realize who Jesus was. Twice in Scripture we see evidence of this, once when Jesus is among the many without food and the other when Philip asks Jesus to show them the Father. We see in Philip a very human man who doubted and questioned like so many of us do. Yet, he became a foundation stone of the Church. We are reminded through Philip's life that holiness and the work that follows is not achieved by human means but is a gift from God. The miracles he performed and the diseases he cured were an external sign of the greater miracle inside of him—the divine power to love like God.

Creator God, we recognize that you call each of us by name. You embrace us and love us as we are. May our knowledge of your unlimited love enable us to face all life's challenges. Amen.

May 14
Matthias, apostle (first century)

Patron of tailors, alcoholics

The Acts of the Apostles tells us that Matthias was chosen after the resurrection to replace Judas. Matthias was one who had been with the other apostles from

Jesus' baptism to his resurrection. The decision was made by drawing lots. It is believed that Matthias ended up in Ethiopia and met his martyrdom by crucifixion or beheading.

D ear God, recognizing that it is you who chose each and everyone one of us out of love, we pray that we can accept Jesus' invitation to follow him. We know that sometimes you ask us to do difficult things, to make difficult choices. You ask us to be courageous and strong and act in ways that are counter-cultural. However, we know the power of your love and the great joy you offer, so we pray for the courage to meet the challenge. We ask this through our Lord and Savior. Amen.

May 15
Isidore, the Farmer, and his wife Maria de la Cabeza (1070-1130)
Patron of farmers, laborers, Madrid

Isidore worked on a farm for a wealthy landowner all his life. He married Maria, and they had one son who died young. Isidore and Maria had a great love for the poor, and it is said that they often supplied them miraculously with food. We see from their life that sainthood does not come from status and that the simple life is conducive to holiness and happiness.

G od of the humble, help us become more faithful people. May we recognize your presence in prayer. May it lead us into a deeper relationship with you. Amen.

May 20
Bernardine of Siena, priest (1380-1444)
Patron of advertisers

Bernardine was the greatest preacher of his time. He calmed strife-torn cities, attacked paganism, and attracted crowds of 30,000 when he preached. He had a keen intuition of the needs of the people, used down-to-earth examples, and radiated boundless energy and joy. He nursed people in the hospital when the plague hit Italy. Following this work he was so exhausted that a fever confined him for several months. At twenty-four he became a Franciscan priest and for twelve years he lived in solitude and prayer. However, his gifts caused him to travel from town to town preaching.

Dear God, we are faced with many decisions in our lives. Give us the strength and insight to make the right choices. We take a moment to pray for families who are suffering today as a result of bad choices that have led to tragedies. May they be granted comfort in friendships and peace in faith. We ask all this through Jesus, our Lord and Savior. Amen.

May 24
Gregory VII, pope (1020-1085)

Before becoming Pope and during his papacy, Gregory fought to free the Church from undue control by civil rulers. He fought against the buying and selling of sacred offices, the unlawful marriage of the clergy, and the idea that kings and nobles control the appointment of church officials. He stressed the role of Bishop of Rome as the vicar of Christ and the visible center of unity in the Church. He reasserted the unity of the whole Church based on Christ.

Dear Jesus, help each of us come to know you better. By entering into a deeper relationship with you may we make your love and your word known throughout the world. Amen.

May 25
Mary Magdalene de Pazzi, virgin (1566-1607)

Mary became a Carmelite nun at the age of sixteen. At seventeen she became critically ill and was allowed to make her vows early. Immediately after, she fell into an ecstasy (union with God) that lasted two hours. This was repeated again for the next forty mornings, after she received communion each morning. These were rich experiences of union with God and God revealed to her marvelous insights into divine truths. Over the next six years five volumes of notes were collected as she explained her ecstasies, her trials and her reform and renewal.

Loving God, this is a very busy time of year. Students and teachers face great pressure as assignments, tests, and presentations are now in full swing. Students try their best to succeed and teachers hope all they have taught has been caught by their students. We ask the intercession of St. Mary Magdalene de Pazzi to maintain a sense of calm balance. Help us recognize that you are always with us offering comfort, direction, and support. Amen.

May 26
Philip Neri, priest (1515-1595)

At an early age Philip went to Rome to devote his life to God. He served thirteen years as a layman engaged in prayer and apostolate. Many laymen formed with him a prayer group and would serve the needy of Rome. He eventually became a priest and it was evident that he had a great gift for recognizing the pretenses and illusions of others. Some of his followers became priests and they lived together in community. This was the beginning of the formation of the Oratory. Philip's advice was sought by many prominent people of his day. He is one of the influential people of the counter-Reformation. He is known for his humility and great spirit of joy.

Creator God, may we serve you with faith and humility. May we use our talents to serve you and be blessed with patience. May our approach to life inspire and encourage others. Amen.

May 27
Augustine of Canterbury, bishop (d. 605)

Augustine and a few monks set out to evangelize the Anglo-Saxons in England. He converted many, constructed a Church and monastery, and as a result, faith began to spread. He did not always meet with success, but he labored patiently. He purified rather than destroyed pagan temples and customs, let pagan rites be taken over into Christian feasts, and retained local customs as much as possible. His work established the foundation for years of conversion that occurred in England after Augustine's death.

God of holiness, grant us the virtues of temperance and wisdom. May we be a patient and holy people. May your will be fulfilled in all we do. Amen.

June 1
Justin, martyr (d. 165)

Patron of philosophers

Justin studied Plato, but later found that Christianity had better answers to the questions about life and existence. After his conversion he became the first Christian philosopher. He felt that philosophy was an educator that could lead one to Christ. In his writings he defended the Christian religion against the attacks and misunderstandings of the pagans. As a result of his faith and his writings in defense of Christianity, Justin was beheaded in Rome in 165.

God of life, you raised Christ your Son from the dead so that we might each have the promise of eternal life. We know that all things are possible to you. Help us at this busy time to be confident in the gifts you have given us. May we be granted the wisdom to apply ourselves completely during this time of final exams and may it bring each of us closer to attaining our dreams. We ask all this through Jesus, our Lord and Savior. Amen.

June 5
Boniface, bishop and martyr (672?-754)

Patron of England

Boniface was an English Benedictine monk who was given the task of reforming and organizing the whole German Church. It had fallen back into paganism and was riddled with error because of uneducated, lax clergy. Boniface was successful but in order to accomplish his mission he did two things: he restored the obedience of the clergy to their bishops in union with the pope and he established many houses of prayer. He also built schools, monasteries, and convents. These were based on Benedictine monasteries. In one of his missionary trips to France, he and fifty-three of his companions were massacred while preparing converts for Confirmation.

God of love, give us the wisdom to achieve your purpose, as St. Boniface did. May we imitate his courage for the sake of your kingdom. Amen.

June 9
Ephrem the Syrian, deacon and doctor (306?-373)

Ephrem was ordained a deacon but declined becoming a priest because he did not believe he was good enough. His prolific writings illustrate his holiness as well as his deep insight and knowledge into the Scriptures. His writings reveal a human-ly sympathetic spirit and a great devotion to the humanity of Jesus and Mary. He also became one of the first to introduce song into the Church's public worship as a means of instruction. He wrote many beautiful and original hymns.

Loving God, as we progress toward the end of this school year, may we find strength in our faith. We know that we are not perfect. Grant us a sympathetic spirit like that of St. Ephrem, and help us be satisfied with doing our best. Amen.

June 11
Barnabas, apostle (first century)

Patron of Cyprus

Barnabas was first called Joseph. He changed his name to Barnabas which means: "son of encouragement." Barnabas comes as close as anyone outside the Twelve to being an apostle. He was a close friend of Paul and introduced Paul to St. Peter and the other apostles. He also defended Paul to the apostles. He was an excellent mediator and was often sent to new churches to represent the mother church of Jerusalem. He and Paul led the Church in Antioch for one year. He preached to many in the gentile world. Barnabas and Paul were very successful at converting the gentile world.

God of wisdom, may teachers know the difference they have made in the lives of students and continue to carry out their duties with wisdom and enthusiasm. May administrators and all support staff who work so hard at keeping this school going know the value of their contributions. Lord, help the staff and administration see that the fruits of their work with the students will be shown in years to come. Amen.

June 13
Anthony of Padua, priest and doctor (1195-1231)

Patron of lost articles, childless women, the poor, harvests, travelers, Portugal

When Anthony saw the slain Franciscan martyrs he was filled with an intense longing to be one of those who die for the Good News. Anthony then joined the Franciscan Order and set out to preach to the Moors. He was stricken with an illness and returned to Italy where he spent most of his time praying, reading the Scriptures, and doing menial tasks. He became recognized as a great man of prayer and a great Scripture and theology scholar. He later preached to the heretics and converted many.

Dear God of all blessings, we give you thanks for our union with Christ. May we be blessed with every spiritual blessing in the heavenly kingdom. Even before the world was made, you had already chosen us to be yours through our union with Christ. Because of your love for us, you made us your children through Jesus—this was your pleasure and purpose. Amen.

June 22
John Fisher, bishop and martyr (1469-1535)

Bishop Fisher was a man of learning, associated with the intellectuals and the political men of his day. He became Chancellor at Cambridge, and bishop at age thirty-five, and worked toward raising the standard of preaching in England. He also was an accomplished preacher and writer and through his writings became a leading theologian in Europe. He paid special attention to the poor and wrote eight books against heresy. He would always hold firm to the truth and the correct action. Along with Thomas More, he defended the validity of Henry VIII's marriage to Queen Catherine and rejected Henry's claim as the supreme head of the Church in England. Like Thomas More, he was condemned and executed.

Dear God, may we make efforts to learn more about you and the Church's position on issues. Whenever we face great pressure, may we not compromise the values that Jesus taught us. May our faith and knowledge of the salvation that is ours provide us with the strength we need in every situation we face. Amen.

June 23
Thomas More, martyr (1478-1535)

Thomas refused to approve Henry VIII's divorce and remarriage and the establishment of the Church of England. Described as "a man for all seasons" More was a literary scholar, eminent lawyer, gentleman, father of four children, and Chancellor of England. He was sent to the Tower and later beheaded. Thomas was an intensely spiritual man who would not go against his conscience, even when it meant his death.

All-powerful God, may we never compromise the values that Jesus taught us, even when we face great pressure. May our faith and knowledge of the salvation that is ours provide us with the strength we need in every situation. Amen.

June 24
Birth of John the Baptist

Today we celebrate the birth of John the Baptist, the son of Elizabeth, a cousin of Jesus. Little did John know, when he was a child, that God was preparing him to be the man who would announce the coming of the Messiah to the Jews. Little did he know that the day would come when he would baptize the Messiah.

Dear God, grant us the gift of patience. When people and society pressure us for the quick fix and the immediate answer, may we take the time we need to search within ourselves for the right answer. May our patience and faith bring us peace. Amen.

June 27
Feast of the Sacred Heart of Jesus

Ask everyone to spend a moment in silent reflection on the great love that Jesus has for each one of us.

June 28
Irenaeus, bishop and martyr (130?-220)

Irenaeus had great patience in investigating information and was very protective of apostolic teachings. He spent much time investigating the gnostic teachings which were influencing many Christians at that time. He wrote five books outlining the gnostic teachings and contrasted them with the teachings of the apostles and the Scriptures. His work contributed greatly to ending the influence of the gnostics. Irenaeus teaches us how important it is to investigate thoroughly in order to arrive at truth.

God of truth, help us always seek the truth as you have taught it to us this past year. May we remain open to the great tasks to which God invites us and may we perform them with joy and hope. Amen.

June 29
Peter, apostle (d. 64) and Paul, apostle (d. 64)

Patron of fishermen

Patron of public relations, the media, missionaries

Peter makes his great confession of faith to Jesus when he says: "You are the Messiah!" Scripture clearly shows Peter as the leader of the apostles, chosen by Jesus to have a special relationship with him. It is to Peter that Jesus says; "You are Rock, and on this Rock I will build my Church."

Paul is converted on the road to Damascus and becomes a great preacher and missionary, traveling throughout the known world to spread the word of God.

Dear God, like Peter and Paul may I repent of my failings and seek ways to bring your gospel to others. May I have the strength to face criticism and even persecution as they did to be true to your teachings. Amen.

CHAPTER FIVE

Scripture Prayers from the Teachings of Jesus

Luke 24:19–21, Luke 2:16–18

Many Israelites believed the messiah would be a great political leader or a general of an army that would free the Jews. Through Jesus, God teaches us that the world is often changed by the most humble and not the most powerful.

Dear Lord, help us see that it is in our weakness that we can find strength, in defeat we can find victory, and by our simple and humble acts we can change people's hearts. May our approach to life and all we do emulate the example of our Lord and Savior, Jesus Christ. Amen.

Matthew 2:7–8

Herod feared the birth of the Infant King and tried to trick the wise men and others into finding this messiah to have him killed. If you take a stand for goodness, if you bring only comfort to others, there will be those who are threatened by your good acts.

Jesus, Messiah, envy and jealousy are emotions that can grab hold of us and destroy us. Free us from these feelings so we can rejoice in the success and good fortune of others. Lord, help us understand these emotions so we can forgive those who are controlled by them. Amen.

Mark 1:4–8

Jesus' cousin, John the Baptist, was a very popular man. However, when Jesus came to him, he was humble and told everyone that this was the messiah they awaited. We will come across many situations in life when we will have to step aside and let someone else use their gifts to contribute great things to the world.

Lord Jesus, we pray for the gift of prudence. We pray that we will know when we are to be humble and allow others to step forward and lead us to great acts. We pray that we will also know when to lead others in building up God's kingdom on earth. Amen.

Matthew 4:1–11

Although Jesus was the messiah, the Son of God, he was tempted. We, too, will be tempted many times in life. To stay in shape spiritually it is important to maintain a strong prayer life, keeping in close contact and good communication with God.

Jesus our teacher, we pray to you for the virtues we need to avoid temptation. We pray for courage to be strong in the face of fear, we pray for strength when we feel weak, we pray for wisdom when our thoughts are filled by the temptation of pleasure. Help us to live faith-filled lives today and always. Amen.

Matthew 2:19–23

Upon returning from their escape from Egypt, Mary, Joseph, and Jesus took up their simple lives in the small town of Nazareth. God chooses each of us in our own way to live our simple lives and yet to have a profound impact on the world.

Lord Jesus, you have gifted us with family, friends, a community, and talents special to us. We thank you for these gifts. We are grateful for the smallest of talents because you have taught us to take these simple things and do good works. Amen.

Matthew 10:1–4

Jesus called twelve apostles; in addition, there were many other men and women who followed Jesus. Jesus calls all of us to a carry out his mission. No matter how big or small we may see our gifts, Jesus sees them as critical to building his kingdom of love on earth.

L ord Jesus, thank you for the gift of your creation, your love, and the gifts you give to each of us. Thank you for inviting us into your kingdom and challenging us to take a part in the building up of this kingdom. You have taught us that there are no limits to what we can do because of the confidence you have in us. Amen.

Mark 1:27–28

Although Jesus didn't begin his brief public ministry until the age of thirty, he worked tirelessly, spreading his message and performing many miracles. His message was so powerful and the miracles he performed were so great that word about him spread quickly among all the Jews in Palestine.

L ord Jesus, you give us the great gifts of health and time. Each of these is so precious. May we not waste time or health on silly behavior. Help us work with enthusiasm, keeping our mind, body, and spirit in condition, in a way similar to an athlete. Amen.

Mark 1:35–39

The son of a carpenter and Jewish by faith, Jesus knew the Old Testament and would preach at every opportunity: in the synagogues, in gatherings in cities, and out in open fields. Some of the Jewish people loved his message; others found parts of his teachings difficult to accept because they were so challenging and different.

J esus Truth, although there were many in your day who could not understand your beautiful message of love, may we understand it today and live a life of tolerance, justice, forgiveness, and compassion because of your message. Amen.

Matthew 5:1–11

The core to Jesus' teaching can be found in Matthew chapters 5 to 7 which we refer to as the Sermon on the Mount. Jesus begins this teaching by giving us the Beatitudes, which are his formula for true happiness.

Lord of life, we are often tempted to seek happiness in all the wrong places. Some people look for it in drugs, some in pleasure, some in power or material wealth. We thank you, Lord, for helping us see that true happiness is found in doing what you promised: being spiritually poor, compassionate, humble, obedient to your will, merciful, pure in heart, peacemakers, and doing what is right and just as God requires. Amen.

Matthew 5:17–20

Jesus delivers a powerful message in the Sermon on the Mount, challenging the Jewish people to take a different stance with regard to anger, sin, divorce, revenge, enemies, prayer, charity, fasting, judging others, and much more. He added a different dimension and asked us to follow not just the law, but to look deeper and follow the spirit of the law.

Lord Jesus, we understand that our righteousness must be of the heart as well as of the mind. We ask for the strength and wisdom to be righteous in act and thought. We also pray that neither fear nor ignorance prevent us from listening with an open ear and open heart to friends and others who have a message that will make us better people. Amen.

Matthew 5:13–16

Like the Jews of Jesus' day, we, too, are threatened by change and messages that challenge the very core of our being. Yet, it is change that makes us alive, makes us grow, and makes us better people. The question is whether we have the courage and fortitude to accept the challenge to change.

Lord Jesus, you taught us that, not only should we not commit murder, but that whoever is angry with his brother will be brought to trial and whoever calls his brother "you good-for-nothing" will be brought to trial. Before we offer any gift to God, may we reconcile and make peace with our brothers and sisters. Lead us to reconciliation and peace. Amen.

Matthew 5:27–30

Many of Jesus' teachings were already a part of the life and faith of the Jewish people, but Jesus developed their meaning still further. He demanded that we not only act properly, but that we have a pure heart and a pure attitude.

Lord Jesus, you taught us about loving our enemies. "You have heard that it was said, 'You shall love your neighbor and hate your enemy.' But I say to you, Love your enemies and pray for those who persecute you, so that you may be children of your Father in heaven; for he makes his sun rise on the evil and on the good, and sends rain on the righteous and on the unrighteous." Fill our hearts with this kind of love. Amen.

Matthew 6:24

We find it difficult to live a life that recognizes that true happiness is not found in material things. Jesus reminds us of this when he tells us that it is impossible to be a slave to two masters: we cannot serve both God and money.

Jesus our teacher, we commit our lives to you, setting aside our desire for material goods. All that we do and all that we are is for you. May we work to build up your kingdom on earth through feeding the hungry, caring for the sick, healing the suffering, and caring for all those in need of our love. Amen.

Matthew 7:1–5

Two very difficult challenges are: not to judge others and to forgive those who persecute us. Jesus is calling us to an attitude and a life that is not only good for others, but also good for ourselves.

Jesus Lord, you taught us: "Do not judge, and you will not be judged; do not condemn, and you will not be condemned. Forgive, and you will be forgiven…. How can you say to your neighbor, 'Friend, let me take out the speck in your eye,' when you yourself do not see the log in your own eye?" (Luke 6:37, 42). Lord, help us listen to your words and give us the strength to follow you. Amen.

Matthew 6:25–34

By performing miracles and healing people, Jesus let the Jewish people know that their sins were forgiven and that their God was a God of mercy who desires that the people be whole. Prayer is a powerful force in healing those who are ill.

Jesus, Lord of life, we call upon you to heal our friends and family members who are ill. We ask that you heal them of their physical as well as their emotional and spiritual brokenness. Heal us of our guilt, our selfishness, and everything that prevents us from being healthy and whole persons. Amen.

Matthew 9:2–8

Jesus healed those who had faith; in addition Jesus calls upon them to have courage once they have been healed. Sometimes we may want healing, but we become comfortable with a lifestyle that involves self-pity. We also fear the responsibilities that come with being healthy again.

Lord Jesus, give us courage. You call us to a better life, you call us to a life that is filled with challenges to give back to the world. Give us the courage, Lord, to walk again, to carve new paths, to adopt new attitudes, and to make a difference in the world. Amen.

Matthew 9:9–13

As we walk through Jesus' ministry we see many things Jesus did that upset the Jews of his time, especially the Pharisees. They could not understand how Jesus would associate with sinners and the outcasts of their society.

Lord of mercy, we pray that we, too, will have the strength you had to reach out and comfort all those who are rejected by our society. We pray for the strength to face the criticism that results from our actions. May people see that your love is given to everyone, that every person is a child of God. Amen.

Matthew 10:5–15

Jesus saw great potential in each of the apostles and he empowered them with gifts to carry out their ministry. Jesus also chooses each of us, and gives us the gifts we need to make a difference in the world.

Jesus our teacher, you have chosen us to spread your love to all people, to live out the mission of building your kingdom, to be an instrument of peace to the world, to be a comfort to those who suffer. Help us discover and develop those gifts in a way that says, "God, you chose me, and I, too, chose you." Amen.

Matthew 10:16–23

Jesus warns those who follow him, that they will be persecuted because of the path they will choose. When we make choices in life for that which is just and right, we will run the risk of being criticized and even persecuted. Jesus reminds us not to be afraid.

Jesus Lord, you taught us: "Do not fear those who kill the body but cannot kill the soul.... Whoever does not take up the cross and follow me is not worthy of me. Those who find their life will lose it, and those who lose their life for my sake will find it." Amen.

Matthew 11:28–30

Sometimes we make the mistake of believing that we can go it alone. All of us need others to lean on. Jesus tells us we can turn to him when we are in need of help.

Dear Lord, you said, "Come to me, all you that are weary and are carrying heavy burdens, and I will give you rest. Take my yoke upon you, and learn from me; for I am gentle and humble in heart, and you will find rest for your souls. For my yoke is easy, and my burden is light." May we turn to you in times of sorrow and difficulty. Amen.

Matthew 12:1–8

Jesus points out that the greatest sins are pride and self-righteousness; attitudes that cause us to look for the sins of others and judge them.

Jesus Lord, when we judge others we offend you. Grant us understanding so that we will not cast judgment on others. For those who are broken, may we be there with kindness and help them find healing. We pray for the kind of mercy you have shown us. Amen.

Matthew 12:9–14

Jesus pointed out to the Pharisees that, as important as the law was, there was nothing more important than kindness and compassion. The law was created to build a greater kingdom, and sometimes the law had to be put aside for a greater good.

Jesus our Way, we pray for an informed conscience, a conscience formed by learning, prayer, and the gifts of the Holy Spirit. We ask for this so that all that we do is done for what is right, for your sake. We also pray for the courage to accept the results of our actions, especially when they are wrong. May we listen to the voice of our conscience and recognize it as God's voice speaking to us. Amen.

Matthew 12:33–37

Jesus points out that to have good fruit you must have a healthy tree. A tree is known by the kind of fruit it bears. What kind of tree are we? To determine this we have to look at our words and actions.

Lord Jesus, every word we speak to each person we meet, every action we do throughout the day, is a reflection of who we are. We wish to bear good fruit, and ask you to send your Spirit into our lives, making our roots good and healthy ones, nourished in prayer. Amen.

Matthew 13:1–8

Jesus' parables were powerful tools in conveying a message because they would invite the listener into the story. In addition, Jesus' parables had many levels of meanings. Everyone who listened received a powerful message at some level or another.

Jesus our teacher, in the parable of the sower you teach us the importance of letting the seed of your Word fall on fertile ground. May we reflect on your teachings and use them in a way that best serves your people and your creation. Amen.

Matthew 14:1–12

It is difficult enough to lose loved ones, but to lose them as a result of injustice, as is the case with John the Baptist, makes a loss even more difficult. Perhaps you know someone who was an innocent and loving person and then died as a result of injustice. This is a difficult reality to accept.

Lord of life, we live in a world that sometimes seems cruel and unjust. We cannot change the entire world, but we can take a stand wherever we witness injustice. May we use our gifts to make every effort to promote justice. Amen.

Matthew 15:21–28

Jesus gave equal status to children, women, the sick, and lepers. He reminded his apostles that he came to those who are ill, who need him. We, too, are called to minister to the broken, to the outcast, to those rejected by society, to find a place in our heart for those who have no place in society.

Lord Jesus, may we see you in every person; the sick, the suffering, the broken, the outcast. All of us are your creation and every person reflects your beauty, your wisdom, and your love. May we carry out your works of mercy for the sick, the hungry, the oppressed, the imprisoned. You have taught us that we are all equally your children. We pray for justice in the world so that all people may be shown the respect they deserve. Amen.

Matthew 16:13–20

Who was Jesus? Some believed he was the Son of God and Messiah prophesied for centuries, others believed he was just another prophet, and some believed he was a blasphemer. Peter believed and proclaimed Jesus to be the Messiah, the Son of the living God. For this, Jesus named Peter the Rock and said it was upon Peter that he would build his Church.

Jesus Lord, help each of us place you at the center of our lives. May we have the faith to live by your message. Amen.

Matthew 16:21–23

Jesus shocked the apostles when he predicted his own death. Some of them would not accept this prophecy.

Jesus Master, you give each of us special gifts. To some you give the gift of prophecy. May our hearts and ears be open so that we can accept the new teachings of great prophets, so we can accept the changes that come with adopting new and better ideas and attitudes, so we can receive a new heart. Amen.

Matthew 18:1–5

Jesus reminds the Jewish people that they must be humble to inherit the kingdom of God. He does this by speaking of children. When ego takes over we lose sight of reality, we distance ourselves from people and we set ourselves up for the greatest of falls.

Jesus, you taught us to always remain humble. You called a child, had him stand in front of your disciples, and said, "Truly I tell you, unless you change and become like children, you will never enter the kingdom of heaven. Whoever becomes humble like this child is the greatest in the kingdom of heaven." May we learn this lesson of seeing ourselves as we really are. Amen.

Matthew 18:6–9

Jesus warns us that to constantly fall into temptation is to lose one's life. It is better to take the painful steps necessary and make the big sacrifices in order to gain control of our life and live it fully.

Jesus our way, we learn from your life that it is possible to conquer temptation. We invite you to be ever present in our life so that we will always find the courage and strength to fight temptation in our life and live in a way that is truly free. Amen.

Matthew 18:10–14

In the parable of the Lost Sheep Jesus tells us that he loves us so much that he will search us out when we go astray. It is hard to believe, but Jesus does love us that much, and he looks out for us when we are lost.

Jesus, Good Shepherd, we desire to always be in your presence. When we feel the touch of your love, we are healed of our brokenness. We are empowered by your love and grace. Give us the strength to remain on the right path and overcome any obstacles we may meet. Amen.

Matthew 18:15–20

Jesus gives to us the power to reconcile with others, to forgive the sin of another, to build up the kingdom through our thoughts and actions. In a world where we often feel powerless, Jesus gives us the opportunity to believe in ourselves and believe that we are capable of accomplishing good things.

Lord Jesus, you fill us with the gift of your love and with the gifts of the Holy Spirit. These are great gifts, and we pray we may use them in ways that best serve the world and all your people. Amen.

Matthew 18:21–22

One of the most difficult things to do in life is to forgive someone who has persecuted or wronged you. Through forgiveness we have the power to actually change our own hearts and the hearts of others.

Jesus Lord, we are all sinners. We know that we have sinned and throughout our lives have said and done things that have hurt others. We ask your forgiveness. We know, Lord, that your mercy and forgiveness will be given to us according to the forgiveness and mercy we give others. Grant us a forgiving heart, Lord, so we may be merciful to others and show our gratitude for the mercy you grant to us. Amen.

Matthew 19:1–9

Jesus saw his relationship with people as a covenant: an unbreakable bond that is free of conditions. A covenant goes beyond a contract or simple friendship and is the kind of relationship that says you are forgiven for all that you have done, and I am always here to accept you and love you when you return to me.

Jesus Lord, we know your covenant love for us. We know that even when we walk away from you, you do not walk away from us. You are with us always, embracing us and waiting for us when we stray. Thank you, Lord, for showing us this kind of love and teaching us about covenant. Amen.

Scripture Prayers from the Teachings of Jesus

Matthew 19:13–15

Jesus was drawn to those who were pure of heart, brought no harm to others, and approached life with a simple faith. Jesus values innocence and purity of heart.

Jesus Lord, as we grow older, we pray we may not lose the purity of mind of our childhood. May we not become entangled in the stereotypes and prejudice of this world. We pray to keep a heart that is pure, a faith that is simple, and a life directed toward doing only what is good. Amen.

Matthew 19:16–22

Jesus told the rich young man that if he wanted to be perfect he had to give up all he had and follow him. When he said this, the man chose to walk away, sad because he could not find the strength to do it.

Jesus our Way, every day we obey your commandments so we can live in a civil society, get along with others, and please you. Sometimes it is difficult to obey these laws, and we need your help so we will do what is right. Give us strength, Lord, when we are most vulnerable to sin. Remind us, through your Spirit, of the suffering caused by disobeying your law. Amen.

Matthew 19:27–30

When Jesus challenges us to give up all that we have to follow him, he is talking about giving up our ego, that is, our desire to rule our own life, without God. Once we can do this, he can teach us how to become his true disciples.

Lord Jesus, we desire to conquer our self more than conquering anything else. May we empty our mind and hearts of all that is against your commandments, so we can be filled with your pure love. We desire this, Lord, and ask you to give us each that kind of courage. With your help, Lord, this can be done and we can be more like you. Amen.

Matthew 20:16

Jesus says, "Many who now are first will be last, and many who now are last will be first." We must have humility if we are going to be open to learning, changing, and making a difference in the world.

Jesus Lord, when we begin to believe that we know it all or have already become as good as possible, please remind us how much we still have to learn and grow, and how much we rely on you. We desire greatness, Lord, and yet we know that to achieve holiness, we must seek your kingdom. Teach us, Lord, so our hearts and minds may remain open to others, to new knowledge, and new heights of spiritual knowledge. Amen.

Matthew 20:20–23

Much of Jesus' teaching refers to the kind of life that will bring heaven here on earth. We can bring heaven to earth by simple acts of kindness and love. We can change the world by doing simple and small acts with great love.

Jesus Lord, help us do frequent acts of kindness for others each day. May we seek to do everything with love. We desire to be a people of hope, believing that what we do builds up your kingdom, so that all people can live in love, harmony, and peace. Amen.

Matthew 20:1–16

Jesus tells the parable of three groups of workers all working different lengths of time but all three getting paid the same amount. Those who worked the longest felt cheated even though they agreed to work all day for the given amount. Perhaps Jesus wanted to remind us of the power of envy and jealousy, which cause us great unhappiness, even when we receive a fair deal in life.

Lord Jesus, teach us to rejoice in everything good that happens to other persons, to be happy for their prosperity and good fortune. When life seems unfair to us and we become ungrateful for the blessings we have been given, teach us, Lord, to be grateful for what we have and to find great joy in the good fortune of others. In this way we will find peace. Amen.

Matthew 20:17–19

With all that Jesus taught the apostles about humility, doing the will of God, and suffering for the kingdom, they still found it difficult to accept when Jesus told them he would be put to death. Sometimes we get so immersed in our own opinions that we refuse to listen to God's warning, even when God has told us many times.

Dear Lord, we come to you with an open heart to receive your love, an open mind to hear your Word, and a willingness to accept all that you say. We hand ourselves over to you on this day and every day, accepting whatever is easy and difficult and doing it all for you, to glorify you. Amen.

Matthew 20:20–28

Over and over Jesus challenges our ego. It is ego that leads to pride and self-righteousness, alienates us from people and the world, and in the end, will cause our unhappiness and destruction.

Jesus our life, you taught us: "Whoever wishes to be great among you must be your servant, and whoever wishes to be first among you must be your slave; just as the Son of Man came not to be served but to serve, and to give his life a ransom for many." May our lives be filled with acts of goodness towards others. Amen.

Matthew 20:29–34

Jesus not only healed physical ailments, he also healed people spiritually, mentally, and emotionally. In every case healing occurred only when the people had faith. For us to overcome obstacles in our life we have to believe that it is possible and that there is that source of love that will help us.

Lord of life, we have faith in your love and in your power. Heal those of us who suffer from physical, mental, emotional, and spiritual illness. Heal us so we may be whole, and in our wholeness better serve you and your people. Amen.

Matthew 21:5

In the gospel of Matthew, Matthew quotes the Old Testament eleven times to prove that Jesus is the Messiah. He demonstrates that Jesus' life matches what the prophets predicted of the upcoming Messiah.

Lord Jesus, we call you Son of God, Son of Man, Savior, and Messiah because we believe that you are the fulfillment of all that the Israelites and humankind needed and desired. You come to this world, fully divine and fully human. Through you we have found promise, hope, truth, life, and salvation. We thank you, Jesus, for being all things to us and for providing us with all that we need. Amen.

Matthew 21:1–11

Zechariah prophesied that the Messiah would enter Jerusalem on a donkey and so he did. Jesus entered Jerusalem on a donkey and the people praised and greeted him, throwing their cloaks and branches on the ground before him.

Lord Jesus, we praise you as prophet and as Savior every moment of every day. We know that each and every moment is eternity to you. We accept you, praise you, proclaim you every moment of our lives. You fill every breath we take and every thought we have because you are our Savior and our life. Amen.

Matthew 21:23–27

Even as the picture of Jesus became clearer to the people of Israel, many did not come to understand that Jesus was the Messiah.

Jesus Messiah, we have come to know you through your Incarnation. You became fully human while remaining fully divine. We pray for the gifts of the Holy Spirit so that as we go through life, we will recognize things as they truly are. Help us, Lord, to recognize truth from deceit, good from bad, right from wrong, purity from corruption. May we see these things clearly so we can experience the fullness and beauty of life. Amen.

Luke 7:43–45

The prophets believed that the Messiah would be a descendent of David and rule Israel as David did. Instead, Jesus taught us that it is not powerful weapons that will free the human person and change the world; it is the power of love.

Lord Jesus, guide us so that the words we use change the world. Guide us so every word we speak is a powerful word of kindness. We sometimes forget the power of the tongue. May the gift of words always be used to uplift the human spirit, recognize the good in others, praise and rejoice in other people's fortune, calm the spirit, and build a world founded on love. Amen.

Matthew 18:21

We keep forgetting that it is the power of the word, the use of a simple pen, that can change the world. The pen can change the world more quickly then the missile.

Lord of life, we see that it is through the spoken word that we can change the heart of another. Help us resist the temptation to use violence or to strike out with anger when kind and forgiving words are needed. Help us control our pride and have us empty ourselves to do what is righteous and wonderful. Amen.

Matthew 21:12–13

When Jesus entered the sacred Temple in Jerusalem, he became angry because they had changed this place of prayer into a house of thieves where there were all kinds of buying and selling.

Lord God, we have infinite reverence for you, our creator. We pray that we may have the strength to avoid using your name in vain, or saying any vile or evil thing about you, or using any place of worship, any sacred place with lack of reverence and respect. May the temptations of this world never control us, causing us to fall into behavior that does not respect you or your creation. Amen.

Matthew 21:18–22

Jesus reminds us that if we do not believe in ourselves and the gifts God has given us, we will accomplish nothing. We cannot move mountains or cross dangerous seas if we do not have faith in him and believe in ourselves.

Lord Jesus, you created each of us with special gifts and the power and ability to do your work. We give you thanks for our hearts that can love, our minds that can think creatively, and our bodies that can do good things. May we use the gifts you have given us, especially the gift of faith, to serve you and your people. Amen.

Matthew 23:1–36

Jesus found pride and self-righteousness to be the greatest of sins. When we look for the sins of others and judge others, we ourselves are guilty of sin.

Jesus our teacher, may we never judge others or speak badly of them. If someone speaks badly of us and others, give us the strength not to react in kind but to respond in a forgiving and compassionate way. Help us not to cast judgment, or to bring judgment and suffering upon another. May all we say and do support our sisters and brothers, and create a better world. Amen.

Matthew 21:28–32

We have mentioned a number of times how radical Jesus' teachings were to the people of his day. The truth makes people uncomfortable with their place in life and challenges them to change.

Jesus Lord, you said to your disciples, "Truly I tell you, the tax collectors and the prostitutes are going into the kingdom of God ahead of you. For John came to you in the way of righteousness and you did not believe him, but the tax collectors and the prostitutes believed him." Jesus, strengthen our faith in you, even when the truth of faith is difficult. Amen.

Matthew 21:14–17

Jesus was infinitely understanding and merciful and could feel the brokenness and pain of those who followed a certain way of life, like tax collectors or beggars. Who are the outcasts in our society?

Lord Jesus, you are all merciful and you teach us mercy. Give us the wisdom to see the story behind every person, the reason behind their actions. May we always be forgiving and merciful, embracing those who suffer, and comforting them with our material as well as spiritual aid. Amen.

Matthew 22:8–10

Jesus picked the most unlikely people to be his followers, to spread the Word, to accomplish great things, and to inherit the kingdom. Look around you; it is those you least suspect who will accomplish the greatest good.

Lord Jesus, give us the eyes to recognize the greatness in every human being. Give us the strength to put our trust in those we would normally call "failures." It is those who appear weak and have gone astray who will do your work, if we believe in them. Amen.

Matthew 21:42–44

You have heard the expression that in weakness there is strength. Jesus was trying to tell us that when you least expect it, you will find greatness and in the people you least expect, you will discover the face of God.

Lord of life, we often find ourselves depressed, lonely, and desperate. Send your Spirit to lift our spirits and give us the gifts of wisdom and fortitude. Lord, we meet your people, a people who appear weak and broken, rejected by society and left abandoned. Send your Spirit to lift them up and fill them with your gifts. Amen.

Matthew 22:1–14

Jesus invites us to the kingdom, as he expresses well in his Parable of the Wedding Feast, but he warns us that just because we are invited does not mean we have earned a place in the kingdom. We have to go prepared, ready to receive him as he receives us.

Lord Jesus, we prepare ourselves for you. We read our Scriptures, do our meditations, acts of charity, and work hard at developing our gifts for your glory. May you find us prepared, Jesus, prepared at all times to be greeted by you and to enter your kingdom. Amen.

Matthew 17:1–13

Besides experiencing the joy that we do in our friendships, we are also called to challenge ourselves and our friends to become better people. We are called to help each other live a life worthy of what God calls us to. In this way friendship becomes a real treasure, and the Lord Jesus will receive glory from you.

Jesus, it would be a wonderful world indeed, if we could treat everyone we meet as a true friend, if we could help each one, and be challenged by them, to be the best we can be and to build your kingdom. Give us the wisdom and courage to do this. Amen.

Matthew 22:15–22

The Pharisees try to trap Jesus when they ask him about paying taxes to Caesar. Jesus answers brilliantly: "Give to Caesar what is Caesar's and to God what is God's." If we are true to ourselves and always make our decisions based on what is good for God's people, we can be confident that we will make the right choices.

Lord our teacher, be with us in those moments of darkness when we have to make the most difficult decisions. Shed your light on us, guide us, and walk with us along that path. Keep us strong and give us the courage to pray and search for the truth. Amen.

Matthew 21:33–41

In the Parable of the Wicked Tenants, Jesus is teaching us something important: that when you take for granted the gifts given to you, you lose all gratitude and live a miserable life. Are we grateful?

Jesus, Lord and Savior, you have given us so many gifts: the gift of life; the ability to think and hope; the ability to laugh and to help others; the beautiful gifts of nature. You have given us all we need to find peace and happiness in this life. May we never take your gifts for granted. May we live a life of gratitude for all the wonders of creation, and never tire of being grateful for every part of life. Amen.

Matthew 23:34–40

To fully appreciate life and to acquire the gifts of wisdom and prudence, Jesus challenges us to rise above the trappings of this world and think in another dimension. We have to turn to prayer, moments of reflection and meditation, and turn our thinking to God to accomplish this level of thought.

Jesus our Way, thank you for the gift of this life and the life you offer in heaven. Although we cannot achieve perfection in this world, we can acquire great knowledge and wisdom if we keep our sights on you. We pray to be free of all things that prevent us from seeing your kingdom and working toward building your kingdom on earth. Amen.

Matthew 23:11–12

Jesus says, "The greatest among you will be your servant. All who exalt themselves will be humbled, and all who humble themselves will be exalted." Jesus challenges us and tells us that great deeds should be done quietly.

Lord Jesus, may we serve your people and do good works, not to be recognized and acclaimed as good, but merely to create a better world; simply to build your kingdom on earth. In everything we do we want to serve others as you served; to love as you loved; to bring peace and healing as you did. Amen.

Matthew 24:36–44

Jesus said many things the people, even his apostles, did not like to hear. Many times in life we will be told things we do not want to hear. If we want to grow in every way and live life to the fullest, we must pay attention to those who are prophets and to our elders who are wise.

Lord Jesus, protect us from ignorance. It is the darkness of ignorance that can lead us to mistakes and even sin. Give us the courage to keep our minds and hearts open to your message, delivered through others. Lord, give us the strength to accept your teachings. As difficult as they may be, may we follow these words of wisdom. Amen.

Matthew 25:1–13

In the Parable of the Ten Bridesmaids Jesus warns us of how important it is to be prepared. In this case, he is telling us to be prepared for the end of time, for judgment day. It is like this with all of life. No matter what we are about to do, we must plan if we want to be successful.

Lord Jesus, we look for you every day. We seek you out in all that we do and all that we are. We search our hearts, examine our deeds, and look into our world, always seeking to find you. You are everywhere and we plan all things with you as our inspiration, our focus, and our goal. We set our sights on you, Jesus. May we plan all our days around our desire to experience you and the peace and joy you offer. Amen.

Matthew 25:14–30

There is little in life that is more discouraging than seeing someone blessed with talent who chooses not to use that talent.

Lord Jesus, teach us not to waste the gifts you have given us. May we recognize the talents we have. May we find the courage and knowledge to use these talents to help others, to build up your kingdom, and to enjoy a fulfilled and happy life. Amen.

Matthew 26:14–16, 69–75

Jesus' best friends turned against him. Peter, his closest apostle, denied he knew Jesus. There will be times when we feel abandoned and even betrayed by those we held closest to us. The question is: Will we be able to forgive them as Jesus did?

Dear Lord, as difficult as it is, we pray for a forgiving heart. May we be able to forgive anyone who hurts us, especially those who betray and persecute us. We pray to forgive as you did, Jesus, because we know that anger, resentment, and revenge are prisons. Forgiveness is the only answer. It is the only way we can truly be free and change the hearts of those who injure us. Amen.

Matthew 28:1–10

The resurrection of Jesus is the final act of victory. Jesus shows us that love, forgiveness, and peace conquer every act of violence and every army. In the end, those who are able to love are the ones who are truly set free and will receive eternal life.

Jesus, our life and resurrection, we pray that we can rise above all the temptations in life that want to imprison and destroy us. We pray that we can be persons of love and bring healing to a broken world. We pray that we always keep our eyes set on the kingdom. May everything that we do and say, each and every day, make you proud and bring us closer to you. Amen.

CHAPTER SIX

Traditional & Contemporary Prayers

Our daily favorites are a group of prayers that have been collected from a number of sources. These prayers are common prayers used for a number of different occasions. Our teenagers love to know and say these prayers in difficult and joyous times. They find that these prayers enrich their faith and help them live out their everyday lives.

Lord's Prayer

Our Father, who art in heaven,
  hallowed be thy name;
Thy kingdom come,
  Thy will be done
  on earth as it is in heaven.
Give us this day our daily bread;
  and forgive us our trespasses
  as we forgive those who trespass against us.
Lead us not into temptation,
  but deliver us from evil.

Doxology

For thine is the kingdom,
  the power and the glory,
  forever and ever. Amen.

Glory be

Glory be to the Father,
  and to the Son,
  and to the Holy Spirit.
As it was in the beginning,
  is now,
  and ever shall be,
  world without end. Amen.

Memorare

Remember, most gracious Virgin Mary,
  that never was it known
  that anyone who fled to your protection,
  implored your help,
  or sought your intercession,
  was left unaided.
Inspired with this confidence,
  I fly to you,
  O Virgin of virgins, my mother.
To you I come, before you I stand,
  sinful and sorrowful.
Mother of the Word incarnate,
  despise not my petitions
  but in your mercy
  hear and answer me. Amen.

Hail, Holy Queen

Hail, holy Queen, mother of mercy,
   our life, our sweetness, and our hope.
To you do we cry,
   poor banished children of Eve;
   to you we send up our sighs,
   mourning and weeping
   in this valley of tears.
Turn then, most gracious advocate,
   your eyes of mercy upon us,
   and after this, our exile,
   show unto us
   the blessed fruit of your womb, Jesus.
O clement, O loving, O kind Virgin Mary.

Hail Mary

Hail, Mary, full of grace,
   the Lord is with you.
Blessed are you among women,
   and blessed is the fruit
   of your womb, Jesus.
Holy Mary, Mother of God,
   pray for us sinners, now
   and at the hour of our death. Amen.

The Angelus

The angel of the Lord declared unto Mary,
and she conceived of the Holy Spirit.
Hail Mary...

Behold the handmaid of the Lord,
Be it done to me according to your word.

Hail Mary...

And the Word was made flesh
and dwelt among us.

Hail Mary...

Pray for us, O holy Mother of God,
that we may be made worthy of the promises of Christ.
Pour forth, we beseech you, O Lord,
your grace into our hearts,
so that we, to whom the incarnation of your Son
was made known by the message of an angel,
may by his passion and cross
be brought to the glory of his resurrection.
We ask this through the same Christ our Lord. Amen.

Morning Offering

Almighty God, we thank you
for the life and light of a new day.
Keep us safe today
and protect us from every evil.
We offer ourselves this day to you
through Jesus Christ your Son.
May your Holy Spirit
make our thoughts, words, and actions
pleasing in your sight.

Grace Before Meals

Bless us, O Lord,
and these your gifts
which we are about to receive
from your bounty,
through Christ our Lord. Amen.

Grace Before Meals

The eyes of all look to you, O Lord,
  to give them their food in due season.
You open wide your hands
  and fill all things with your blessings,
  through Christ our Lord. Amen.

Grace After Meals

We give you thanks, Almighty God,
  for all your gifts
  which we have received,
  through Christ our Lord. Amen.

Grace After Meals

For these and his many mercies,
may the Lord's name be blessed,
now and forever,
  through Christ our Lord. Amen.

Act of Contrition

O my God, I am heartily sorry
  for having offended you,
  and I detest all my sins
  because of your just punishments
  but most of all because they offend you, my God,
  who are all good
  and deserving of all my love.
I firmly resolve
  with the help of your grace
  to confess my sins,
  to do penance, and to amend my life. Amen.

Confiteor

I confess to almighty God,
to Blessed Mary ever virgin,
to Blessed Michael the archangel,
to Blessed John the Baptist,
to the holy apostles Peter and Paul,
and to all the saints,
that I have sinned exceedingly
in thought, word and deed,
through my fault,
through my fault,
through my most grievous fault.
Therefore I beseech
Blessed Mary ever virgin,
Blessed Michael the archangel,
Blessed John the Baptist,
the holy apostles Peter and Paul,
and all the saints,
to pray to the Lord our God for me.

Act of Faith

O my God, I firmly believe
that you are one God
in three divine Persons,
Father, Son, and Holy Spirit.
I believe that your divine Son became man
and died for our sins,
and that he will come to judge
the living and the dead.
I believe these and all the truths
which the holy Catholic Church teaches
because you have revealed them,
who can neither deceive nor be deceived.

Act of Hope

O God, you have given us Jesus
  to be our supreme high priest.
Help us never let go of the faith
  which he has given us.
We hope in him
  because he felt our weaknesses with us
  and was tempted in every way that we are,
  although he was without sin.
Give us his spirit of trust
  that we may approach your throne of grace,
  confident in your mercy.

Act of Love

O God, we believe that you are love
  and that you love us.
Help us to live in love
  that we may live in you and you in us.
Send us your spirit of love
  that we may love as Jesus loved,
  for he has taught us
  that we cannot love you
  if we do not love one another.

Apostles Creed

I believe in God, the Father Almighty,
  Creator of heaven and earth.
I believe in Jesus Christ,
  his only Son, our Lord,
  who was conceived by the Holy Spirit,
  born of the Virgin Mary,
  suffered under Pontius Pilate,

was crucified, died, and was buried.
He descended into hell;
 the third day he arose again from the dead;
He ascended into heaven and is seated
 at the right hand of the Father.
He will come again
 to judge the living and the dead.
I believe in the Holy Spirit,
 the holy Catholic Church,
 the communion of saints,
 the forgiveness of sins,
 the resurrection of the body,
 and life everlasting. Amen.

St. Francis' Peace Prayer

Lord, make me an instrument of your peace.
Where there is hatred let me sow love;
 where there is injury, pardon;
 where there is doubt, faith;
 where there is despair, hope;
 where there is darkness, light;
 and where there is sadness, joy.
O Divine Master,
 grant that I may not so much seek
 to be consoled, as to console,
 to be understood, as to understand,
 to be loved, as to love.
For it is in giving that we receive,
 it is in pardoning that we are pardoned,
 and it is in dying that we are born to eternal life. Amen.

Divine Praises

Blessed be God.
Blessed be his holy name.
Blessed be Jesus Christ, true God and true man.
Blessed be the name of Jesus.
Blessed be his most sacred Heart.
Blessed be his most precious Blood.
Blessed be Jesus in the most holy sacrament of the altar.
Blessed be the Holy Spirit, the paraclete.
Blessed be the great Mother of God, Mary most holy.
Blessed be her holy and Immaculate Conception.
Blessed be her glorious Assumption.
Blessed be the name of Mary, virgin and mother.
Blessed be St. Joseph, her most chaste spouse.
Blessed be God in his angels and in his saints.

Anima Christi

Soul of Christ, make me holy.
Body of Christ, save me.
Blood of Christ, inebriate me.
Water from the side of Christ,
Wash me clean.
Passion of Christ, strengthen me.
Kind Jesus, hear me.
Hide me within your wounds.
Let me never be separated from you.
Defend me from evil.
In the hour of my death
  call me to yourself,
  that with your saints I may praise you
  in everlasting life. Amen.

Prayer Before a Crucifix

Good and dearest Jesus,
  I kneel before you,
  beseeching and praying to you
  with all my heart and soul
  to engrave deep and living signs
  of faith, hope, and love upon my heart,
  with true repentance for my sins
  and a firm resolve to make amends.
I ponder your five wounds,
  dwelling upon them with compassion,
  and recall the words
  the prophet David spoke long ago about you:
  "They have pierced my hands and feet;
  they have numbered all my bones."

Grail prayer

Lord Jesus,
I give you my hands to do your work.
I give you my feet to go your way.
I give you my eyes to see as you do.
I give you my tongue to speak your words.
I give you my mind that you may think in me.

Above all, I give you my heart
  that you may love in me your Father
  and all mankind.
I give you my whole self that
  you may grow in me,
  so that it is you, Lord Jesus,
  who will live and work and pray in me.

Prayer to the Holy Spirit

Come, Holy Spirit, fill the hearts of your faithful
and kindle in them the fire of your love.
Send forth your Spirit, O Lord,
and renew the face of the earth.
O God, on the first Pentecost
you instructed the hearts of those who believe in you
by the light of the Holy Spirit.
Under the inspiration of the same Spirit,
give us a desire for what is right and true
and a continuing sense of his joy,
bringing presence and power.
We ask this through Christ our Lord. Amen.

The Prayer of the Dead

Eternal rest grant to him/her, O Lord,
And let perpetual light shine upon him/her.
May his/her soul and the souls of all the faithful departed,
through the mercy of God, rest in peace. Amen.

The Rosary

Here is one way to pray the mysteries of the rosary:

The Joyful Mysteries are prayed on Monday and Saturday;
The Sorrowful Mysteries are prayed on Tuesday and Friday;
The Glorious Mysteries are prayed on Wednesday and Sunday;
The Luminous Mysteries are prayed on Thursday.

Joyful Mysteries

First Joyful Mystery: The Annunciation
The Word of God becomes flesh in the womb of the Virgin Mary.

Second Joyful Mystery: The Visitation
Mary visits her cousin Elizabeth, mother of John the Baptist who will announce the coming of Christ.

Third Joyful Mystery: The Nativity
Jesus is born in a stable in Bethlehem.

Fourth Joyful Mystery: The Presentation in the Temple
Jesus is presented in the temple.

Fifth Joyful Mystery: The Finding of Our Lord in the Temple
Jesus is found by his parents among the teachers of God's law.

Sorrowful Mysteries

First Sorrowful Mystery: The Agony in the Garden
Jesus prays that his Father's will be done.

Second Sorrowful Mystery: The Scourging at the Pillar
Pilate orders Jesus to be scourged.

Third Sorrowful Mystery: The Crowning with Thorns
The soldiers mock and insult Jesus, crowning him king of the Jews.

Fourth Sorrowful Mystery: The Carrying of the Cross
Jesus is led out of Jerusalem to die on the hill of Golgotha.

Fifth Sorrowful Mystery: The Crucifixion
Jesus dies on the cross and is buried.

Glorious Mysteries

First Glorious Mystery: The Resurrection
Jesus is raised from the dead.

Second Glorious Mystery: The Ascension
Jesus is taken up into the Father's glory.

Third Glorious Mystery: The Descent of the Holy Spirit upon the Apostles
As he had promised, Jesus sends the spirit to his disciples.

Fourth Glorious Mystery: The Assumption
Mary enters her Son's heavenly glory.

Fifth Glorious Mystery: The Crowning of Mary as Queen of Heaven and Earth
Mary becomes a special sign of the victory all share in Christ.

Mysteries of the Light/The Luminous Mysteries

These mysteries we proclaimed by Pope John Paul II in 2002. Each of the mysteries is a revelation of the kingdom present in the person of Jesus.

First Luminous Mystery: Baptism in the Jordan
Jesus is baptized. His Father in heaven declares Jesus the beloved Son.

Second Luminous Mystery: Wedding at Cana
Thanks to the intervention of Mary, Christ changes water into wine and opens the hearts of the disciples to faith.

Third Luminous Mystery: Proclamation of the Kingdom
*Jesus proclaims the coming of the kingdom
and forgives the sins of all who draw near to him.*

Fourth Luminous Mystery: Transfiguration on Mount Tabor
Jesus commands the apostles to listen to him and to prepare to experience with him the passion so to come to new life in the resurrection.

Fifth Luminous Mystery: Institution of the Eucharist
Christ offers his body and blood as food under the signs of bread and wine and testifies to his love for humanity, offering salvation in his sacrifice.

Prayer after the Rosary

God, your only begotten son,
    by his life, death, and resurrection,
    has obtained for us the rewards of eternal life;
    grant we beseech you,
    that meditating on these mysteries
    of the holy rosary of Blessed Mary, his mother,
    we may imitate what they contain
    and obtain what they promise,
    through Christ our Lord. Amen.

The Stations of the Cross

First station: Jesus is condemned to death

We adore you, O Christ, and we praise you,
because by your holy cross you have redeemed the world.

Jesus, scourged and crowned with thorns, was unjustly condemned to die on the cross. But he accepted this condemnation in order to save us and all the world from sin and death.

Second station: Jesus takes up his cross

We adore you, O Christ, and we praise you,
because by your holy cross you have redeemed the world.

Jesus freely chose to suffer and die for us. Help us love in this same way, willing to suffer and to offer our suffering for others.

Third station: Jesus falls the first time

We adore you, O Christ, and we praise you,
because by your holy cross you have redeemed the world.

It is said that Jesus stumbled under the weight of the cross and the sins of the world. Yet he continued on, encouraging us to rise up when we falter and fail.

Fourth station: Jesus meets his mother

We adore you, O Christ, and we praise you,
because by your holy cross you have redeemed the world.

The Son of God met the mother of all humanity on the way of the cross. Sharing her compassion, we are to see the Lord present in all who suffer, for they are God's chosen ones.

Fifth station: Jesus is helped by Simon of Cyrene

We adore you, O Christ, and we praise you,
because by your holy cross you have redeemed the world.

Even in the midst of the worst suffering and cruelty, the spirit of love is at work. May we always be prompted by the Spirit to assist those around us in need, for what we do for another, we do for the Lord.

Sixth station: Veronica wipes Jesus' face with her veil

We adore you, O Christ, and we praise you,
because by your holy cross you have redeemed the world.
Veronica wiped the face of Jesus with her veil, and found there the miraculous likeness of the Lord. By responding to Jesus present in our midst, we ourselves take on God's likeness.

Seventh station: Jesus falls the second time

We adore you, O Christ, and we praise you,
because by your holy cross you have redeemed the world.
Although Jesus was overwhelmed by the weight of the cross, he continued on his way. We, too, are called to persevere on our journey of faith, no matter how futile our efforts seem, because our journey is his.

Eighth station: Jesus speaks to the women of Jerusalem

We adore you, O Christ, and we praise you,
because by your holy cross you have redeemed the world.
The women of Jerusalem wept for Jesus but he said to them: "Weep not for me but for yourselves and your children." The cross of Christ always calls us to repentance—to change our hearts every day of our lives.

Ninth station: Jesus falls a third time

We adore you, O Christ, and we praise you,
because by your holy cross you have redeemed the world.
Even though Jesus may have fallen, for he was like us in all things but sin, he found the strength and courage to continue on. He gives us the same strength and courage to share with him in the world's redemption.

Tenth station: Jesus is stripped of his garments

We adore you, O Christ, and we praise you,
because by your holy cross you have redeemed the world.
The executioners stripped Jesus and took his clothes, gambling over who would keep them. We must also be ready to be stripped of all we have and own, that God may truly make us his.

Eleventh station: Jesus is nailed to the cross

We adore you, O Christ, and we praise you,
because by your holy cross you have redeemed the world.
As they crucified Jesus, he prayed, "Father, forgive them; they know not what they do." Crucified with Jesus, we are called by his spirit to bring forgiveness and reconciliation to all the world.

Twelfth station: Jesus dies on the cross

We adore you, O Christ, and we praise you,
because by your holy cross you have redeemed the world.
Jesus breathed forth his spirit, praying, "Into your hands, father, I commit my Spirit." Through Christ's suffering and death, God brought healing and unity to the world. To share in the Father's healing love, we surrender our life and death into his hands.

Thirteenth station: Jesus is taken down from the cross

We adore you, O Christ, and we praise you,
because by your holy cross you have redeemed the world.
It was accomplished. Joseph of Arimathea took Jesus' body down from the cross, while the women who followed Jesus watched and waited. We, too, must trust, waiting in vigilance and patience, for God to work his wonderful deeds even in our suffering and death.

Fourteenth station: Jesus is laid in the tomb

We adore you, O Christ, and we praise you,
because by your holy cross you have redeemed the world.
The body of Jesus is wrapped in a shroud and laid in a tomb hewn out of rock. It was sealed with a stone, and the women prepared spices with which to anoint his body. But God brought forth life from death, light from darkness—the same life and light he brings forth in us.

Fifteenth station: Jesus rises from the dead

We adore you, O Christ, and we praise you,
because by your resurrection you offer new life.
Jesus' resurrection confirms that he conquered evil and sin and that he offers all of us the opportunity to live with him forever in paradise. May we always be filled with the spirit of his love and the hope of the resurrection.

Alternate prayers for the Way of the Cross
First station: Jesus is condemned to death

Dear Jesus, you made the journey of your death with confidence and love. May your acceptance and resignation encourage us to deal with the challenges that life presents to us. May your love and example give us the strength and determination to face whatever comes. Amen.

Second station: Jesus takes up his cross

Dear Jesus, may we take up our daily cross as you took yours. We deal with boredom, disappointments, arguments, and frustration. May we know that in carrying our own cross you are with us. Help us gain strength and comfort knowing that we journey together. Amen.

Third station: Jesus falls the first time

Dear Jesus, carrying your cross was difficult for you and you fell. Help us to accept the times in our life when we are weak. We know that being human involves being weak. However, we take comfort in knowing that you are always there for us. Amen.

Fourth station: Jesus meets his mother

Dear Jesus, we witness and share in Mary's suffering as she meets you carrying your cross. What faith Mary displayed, in watching you, her own son, suffer. However, she knew that God's will must be done and that your passion and death must take place. When we are challenged by seeing those around us suffer, our friends, our family, may we be granted similar strength. May our faith in you and our joy in your resurrection continue to provide us with hope. Amen.

Fifth station: Jesus is helped by Simon of Cyrene

Dear Jesus, help us recognize that every time we assist someone in the simplest of tasks—food drives, clothing drives, or volunteering in any way—we are doing what Simon did. There are always people, every day, every minute, who could benefit by our help. May we be willing to reach out and help others carry their crosses. Amen.

Sixth station: Veronica wipes Jesus' face with her veil

Dear Jesus, help us see your face in all those with whom we associate. Give us the courage and willingness to sacrifice ourselves to help others in need. May your acts of love and compassion live in us. May we have the courage and willingness to care for those who are in need of our love. Amen.

Seventh station: Jesus falls the second time

Dear Jesus, grant us the courage and strength we need to get through the day. When failure, sadness, and loneliness weigh us down, stretch out your hand and lift us up. Help us to never give up, just as you never gave up. Help us struggle on and succeed no matter how difficult the day is. We know, Lord, that with you all things are possible. Your life was living testimony of that. Amen.

Eighth station: Jesus speaks to the women of Jerusalem

Dear Jesus, your compassion in your passion brings tears to our eyes. Teach us to imitate your ways, your love, and your understanding. We, too, have difficult burdens. However during these times may we not get lost in our own problems. May your example of self-sacrifice and love guide and inspire us always. Amen.

Ninth station: Jesus falls a third time

Dear Jesus, you demonstrated to us in your passion that our will and our convictions cannot be taken from us. We can hold onto what we value and believe and no one can take this from us. May we be granted courage like yours, and never compromise ourselves because of pressure or embarrassment. Amen.

Tenth station: Jesus is stripped of his garments

Dear Jesus, you are the king of the world, who is humbled before the crowds when you are stripped of your clothes after you have carried your cross. You possess nothing except God's love and will. Help us be humble. Help us offer all that we have to you. Steer us away from the materialism of this world and lead us to the glory of your kingdom. Amen.

Eleventh station: Jesus is nailed to the cross

Dear Jesus, we look at your suffering and wonder, are we worth that much? We ask ourselves: "What can we do in return for what you have done for us?" Amen.

Twelfth station: Jesus dies on the cross

Dear Jesus, you gave your life for us. How beautiful and deep your love is. May we be filled with your love and look forward to the joy and peace that is promised to us when we join you in heaven. Amen.

Thirteenth station: Jesus is taken down from the cross

Dear Jesus, you breathed your last breath. Your pain is over. Thank you for the gift of yourself to us. Amen.

Fourteenth station: Jesus is laid in the tomb

Dear Jesus, you are laid to rest. The sacrifice is now complete. Amen.

Fifteenth station: Jesus rises from the dead

Dear Jesus, we celebrate with great joy the promise of eternal life and we long to be with you! Amen.

Footprints in the Sand

One night a man had a dream. He dreamed he was walking along the beach with the Lord. Across the sky flashed scenes from his life. For each scene, he noticed two sets of footprints in the sand; one belonged to him, and the other to the Lord.

When the last scene of his life flashed before him, he looked back at the footprints in the sand. He noticed that many times along the path of his life there was only one set of footprints. He also noticed that it happened at the very lowest and saddest times in his life. This really bothered him and he questioned the Lord about it.

"Lord, you said that once I decided to follow you, you would walk with me all the way. But I have noticed that during the most troublesome times in my life, there is only one set of footprints. I don't understand why, when I needed you most, you would leave me."

The Lord replied, "My precious, precious child, I love you. During your times of trial and suffering, when you see only one set of footprints in the sand, it was then that I carried you."

— Author Unknown

Slow Me Down, Lord

Give me, amid the confusion of the day, the calmness of the everlasting hills. Break the tensions of my nerves and muscles with the soothing music of the singing streams that live in my memory. Help me know the magical, restoring power of relaxation. Teach me the art of taking minute vacations, of slowing down to look at a flower, to chat with a friend, to pat a dog, to read a few lines from a good book.

Remind me each day of the fable of the hare and the tortoise, that I may know that the race is not always to the swift. There is more the life than increasing its speed. Let me look upward into the branches of the towering oak and know that it grew great and strong because it grew slowly and well. Slow me down, Lord, and inspire me to send my roots deep into the soil of life's enduring values that I may grow toward the stars of my greater destiny. Amen.

— Richard Cardinal Cushing

Meditation

God has created me to do him some definite service; he has committed some work to me, which he has not committed to another. I have my mission—I may never know it in this life, but I shall be told it in the next. I am a link in the chain, a bond of connection between persons. He has not created me for naught. I shall do good, I shall do his work. I shall be an angel of peace, a preacher of truth in my own place while not intending it—if I do but keep his Commandments.

Therefore I will trust him. Whenever, wherever I am, I can never be thrown away. If I am in sickness, my sickness may serve him; in perplexity, my perplexity may serve him; if I am in sorrow, my sorrow may serve him. He does nothing in vain. He knows what he is about. He may take away my friend; he may throw me among strangers. He may make me feel desolate, make my spirit sink, hide my future from me—still he knows what he is about.

— John Cardinal Newman

Excerpt from Nelson Mandela's Presidential Inaugural Speech

Our deepest fear is not that we are inadequate. Our deepest fear is that we are powerful beyond measure. It is our light, not our darkness, that most frightens us. We ask ourselves, who am I to be brilliant, gorgeous, talented, and fabulous? Actually, who are you not to be?

You are a child of God. Your playing small doesn't serve the world. There's nothing enlightened about shrinking so that other people won't feel insecure around you. We are born to make manifest the glory of God that is within us. It's not just in some of us; it's in everyone. And as we let our own light shine, we consciously give other people permission to do the same. As we are liberated from our fear, our presence automatically liberates others.

Mother Teresa's Prayer

People are often unreasonable,
  illogical and self-centered;
Forgive them anyway.

If you are kind,
  people may accuse you of selfish motives;
Be kind anyway.

If you are successful,
  you will win some false friends and some true enemies;
Succeed anyway.

If you are honest and frank,
  people may cheat you;
Be honest and frank anyway.

What you spend years building,
  someone could destroy overnight;
Build anyway.

If you find serenity and happiness,
  they may be jealous;
Be happy anyway.

The good you do today,
  people will often forget tomorrow;
Do good anyway.

Give the world the best you have,
  and it may never be enough;
Give the world the best you have anyway.

You see, in the final analysis,
  it is between you and God;
It never was between you and them anyway.

Shaping Tomorrow

Disturb us, Lord, when
  we are too well pleased with ourselves;
When our dreams have come true
  because we have dreamed too little;
When we have arrived safely
  because we have sailed too close to the shore.

Disturb us, Lord, when
  with the abundance of things we possess
  we have lost our thirst for waters of life;
Having fallen in love with life,
  we have ceased to dream of eternity;
And in our efforts to build a new earth,
  we have allowed our vision of the new heaven to dim.

Disturb us, Lord to dare more boldly
  to venture on wider seas
  where storms will show your mastery,
  where losing sight of land,
  we shall find the stars.
We ask you to push back
  the horizons of our hope;
  and to push us in the future
  in strength, courage, hope and love.

— Sir Francis Drake